Faces in a Crowd is a book of poems about people – the anonymous man in the street who passes by unnoticed, the prominent figures of public life and the people who play their roles of postman, librarian, salesman or lavatory attendant. And then there are the faces – the old familiar faces of family and friends, and the unforgettable faces of strangers glimpsed in trains or first-storey windows . . .

Here are people as others see them and as they see themselves. In a collection which includes work by John Betjeman, Ben Jonson, Wendy Cope, Brian Patten and Maya Angelou, no face can be forgotten.

Anne Harvey has enjoyed poetry since childhood and is now well known as an anthologist and for her poetry readings in schools, theatres, on TV and radio. She writes for the press, and directs PEGASUS, a company of actors presenting literary programmes.

Also edited by Anne Harvey

OF CATERPILLARS, CATS AND CATTLE
A PICNIC OF POETRY
POETS IN HAND: A QUINTET OF POETS
SIX OF THE BEST

for older readers
IN TIME OF WAR

Faces
in a Crowd

Poems about People

Edited by Anne Harvey

PUFFIN BOOKS

To my daughter
Charlotte
Another collector of people

PUFFIN BOOKS

Published by the Penguin Group
Penguin Books Ltd, 27 Wrights Lane, London w8 5tz, England
Viking Penguin, a division of Penguin Books USA Inc.
375 Hudson Street, New York, New York 10014, USA
Penguin Books Australia Ltd, Ringwood, Victoria, Australia
Penguin Books Canada Ltd, 2801 John Street, Markham, Ontario, Canada l3r 1b4
Penguin Books (NZ) Ltd, 182–190 Wairau Road, Auckland 10, New Zealand

Penguin Books Ltd, Registered Offices: Harmondsworth, Middlesex, England

First published by Viking 1990
Published in Puffin Books 1991
10 9 8 7 6 5 4 3 2 1

This collection copyright © Anne Harvey, 1990
All rights reserved

The Acknowledgements on pages 164–167 constitute an extension of this copyright page.

Printed in England by Clays Ltd, St Ives plc
Filmset in Linotron Sabon

Faces in a Crowd: Introduction

I've always collected people and am fascinated by them, the way they look, dress, talk, behave. I like watching them on journeys, in restaurants and at public gatherings, and inventing lives for them probably far removed from fact. As Wordsworth said: 'The face of every one that passes by me is a mystery.'

For most of my life I've collected poetry too. As a schoolgirl I would sit in my room for hours copying poems into rather dull green exercise books, deaf to parental cries of 'Fresh air and a nice walk!' Making anthologies has remained a favourite pursuit, although publishing them leads to cries of 'Why didn't you include such-and-such?' and 'You might have found a few more funny ones!'

It's a tricky business, choice. Some poems cry out to be included; others must be read and re-read before they fall into place. Compilers have to guard against clumping a bunch of their favourites together and hoping for the best. Just as writing a poem can take weeks, months of re-working, so too can the piecing together of a poetry collage.

One particular poem seemed to start this collection. A. S. J. Tessimond's *The Man in the Bowler Hat* has always haunted me, summing up so well the little man, the unnoticed one, 'the man they label Little lest one day I dare to grow.' This man is also an individual. He has been an adored baby, a child, a young man; he is perhaps a husband, a father; he will grow old, die. Passers-by know nothing of his dreams. Using him as a centre-piece, I've chosen poems about people in various phases and situations in their lives. Each of them, like each one of us, is highly important to family and friends, but insignificant when part of a queue, a classroom, or an audience.

Poems behave differently in different settings. A poem can lie dormant for years in a poet's Collected Works, then suddenly spring to life when singled out in an anthology . . . like people drawn from a crowd.

All editors want their collections to be fresh and original, and not to overlap other anthologies. I spend a great amount of time searching in libraries and on other people's bookshelves; I pick my friends' brains, pore through poetry magazines for new ideas. Sometimes a half-remembered phrase hovers in my mind and won't go away, then I can't rest until I've recaptured the whole poem.

The shaping and development of a collection is important to me, and I like to plan my books to be read straight through. Poems are placed side by side for a reason: in the sections The Child's Tale and 11 Plus, the children's ages rise from 0 to 21. Some poems turn out to relate to each other, unexpectedly echoing an idea, a word or phrase.

Of course it's possible to open the book anywhere at random and read a poem out of context. Anthologies work both ways. A writer called Sir Walter Raleigh, not the one who threw his cloak across a muddy puddle for Queen Elizabeth I, wrote in his *Wishes of an Elderly Man*:

> I wish I loved the Human Race;
> I wish I loved its silly face;
> I wish I loved the way it walks;
> I wish I loved the way it talks;
> And when I'm introduced to one
> I wish I thought WHAT JOLLY FUN!

There must be times when we've all shared that point of view; most of the time I continue to enjoy people in life and in poetry.

Anne Harvey

Contents

11 Plus

A Job of Some Sort

Strangers on a Train

Unforgettable – That Face

The Family Face

The Lives of Other People

Only One of Me

The Old Familiar Faces

A Stranger Here

You Being Born

I saw you born.
It was remarkable.
You shot out from between your mother's legs
like a rugby ball from a scrum
and the stocky Geordie midwife caught you neatly
and cried 'Whoops! She's come!'

You had a wrinkled jammy head
and spasmy legs like a portly frog's.
From your belly button a white root waved
that had fed you all the months you'd grown

and ripened in your mother's womb.
And let me tell you – I'm ashamed –
I forget your mother completely – she had been
those things to me that one day you'll discover
in someone else, and think 'God, this is it!'
– My sweetheart, my warm dream, my red hot lover –

But for those moments, as the doctor
shoved cotton wool up your flat nose
and swabbed your eyes and cleaned your bum
I forgot completely all my life and love
and watched you like a pool of growing light
and whispered to myself 'She's come! She's come!'

BRIAN JONES

Infant Sorrow

My mother groaned! my father wept.
Into the dangerous world I leapt;
Helpless, naked, piping loud;
Like a fiend hid in a cloud.

Struggling in my father's hands:
Striving against my swaddling bands:
Bound and weary I thought best
To sulk upon my mother's breast.

WILLIAM BLAKE

from The Salutation

These little limbs,
These eyes and hands which here I find,
These rosy cheeks wherewith my life begins,
Where have ye been? Behind
What curtain were ye from me hid so long!
Where was, in what abyss, my speaking tongue?

When silent I
So many thousand, thousand years
Beneath the dust did in a chaos lie,
How could I smiles or tears,
Or lips or hands or eyes or ears perceive?
Welcome ye treasures which I now receive.

I that so long
Was nothing from eternity,

Did little think such joys as ear or tongue
    To celebrate or see:
Such sounds to hear, such hands to feel, such feet,
Beneath the skies on such a ground to meet.

            From dust I rise,
    And out of nothing now awake;
These brighter regions which salute mine eyes,
    A gift from God I take.
The earth, the seas, the light, the day, the skies,
The sun and stars are mine, if those I prize.

            A stranger here
    Strange things doth meet, strange glories see;
Strange treasures lodged in this fair world appear
    Strange all and new to me.
But that they mine should be, who nothing was,
That strangest is of all, yet brought to pass.

                    THOMAS TRAHERNE

My Baby Has No Name Yet

My baby has no name yet;
like a new-born chick or a puppy,
my baby is not named yet.

What numberless texts I examined
at dawn and night and evening over again!
But not one character did I find,
which is as lovely as the child.

Starry fields of the sky,
or heap of pearls in the depth,
Where can the name be found, how can I?

My baby has no name yet;
like an unnamed bluebird or white flowers
from the farthest land for the first time
I have no name for this baby of ours.

KIN-NAM-JO
(translated by Ko Won)

To C. F. H. on Her Christening-Day

Fair Caroline, I wonder what
You think of earth as a dwelling-spot,
And if you'd rather have come, or not?

Today has laid on you a name
That, though unasked for, you will claim
Lifelong, for love or praise or blame.

May chance and change impose on you
No heavier burthen than this new
Care-chosen one your future through!

Dear stranger here, the prayer is mine
That your experience may combine
Good things with glad. . . . Yes, Caroline!

THOMAS HARDY

On the Birth of His Son

Families, when a child is born
Want it to be intelligent.

I, through intelligence,
Having wrecked my whole life,
Only hope the baby will prove
Ignorant and stupid.
Then he will crown a tranquil life
By becoming a Cabinet Minister.

SU TUNG-P'O
(translated by Arthur Waley)

from After the Christening

Come along, everybody, see the pretty baby,
Such a pretty baby ought to be adored.
Come along, everybody, come and bore the baby,
See the pretty baby, begging to be bored.

Hurry, hurry, Aunt Louise,
Silly names are sure to please.
Bother what the baby thinks!
Call her Kitchy-kitch and Binks,
Call her Wackywoo and Snookums,
Just ignore her dirty lookums,
Who than she is fairer game
For every kind of silly name?
Baby cannot answer back,
Or perhaps an aunt she'd lack.

Come along, everybody, isn't she a darling?
Such a little darling ought to be enjoyed.
Come along, everybody, let's annoy the baby,
Such a darling darling begs to be annoyed.

Cousin Charles was always chummy;
He's about to poke her tummy.
Grandpa almost chokes on chuckles,
Tickling with his beard her knuckles;
All of Granny's muscles ache
From half an hour of patty-cake;
God-mamma with glee begins
A noisy count of baby's chins;
God-papa with humor glows
Playing piggie with her toes.
See the happy prideful parents,
Do they think of interference?
Certainly not, while baby gives
Such wholesome fun to relatives.

Up and at her, everybody, at the pretty baby,
Tell her she's a dumpling, tell her she's a dear.
Everybody knows the way to woo a baby —
Tickle her and pinch her and yodel in her ear.

OGDEN NASH

Sister

'. . . someone for you to play with.'
But I could tell she'd be
useless at throwing, or bricks,
no good at pretending.

'Isn't she sweet?' Couldn't they see
she was yellow, creased, spotty,
an unfinished frog, a leaky
croaky cry-for-nothing?

'Be gentle now!' But I was
doing what they said, playing.
My best doll's bonnet
fitted her floppy beetroot head.

She smelled of powdered egg.
They warmed her vests.
She slept against my mother's skin.
'How do you like her?' Send her back.

                CAROLE SATYAMURTI

Rocking Horse

My brother looks cold in the cot,
whose sticky rail, scarred by my first teeth,
tastes of chair legs,

where I spied on shadows
flitting round patterns in the wallpaper,
whose colours ripened in the sun,

where I fingernailed flakes of yellow and red
from the Mickey Mouse transfers above me,
where it felt so warm

and smelled of comfortable things
that I can't have now
in this arid bed I'm scared of falling from.

My brother looks cold,
so I'll cover his feet with my pillow
his body with my Sunday coat.

It shrinks him to a thumb-sucking doll
whom carefully I drape
with hairy blankets from the drawer,

cushions from the wicker chair,
my tainted rubber sheet.
It is quiet.

I topple the rocking horse into the cot,
peep at the scarlet face,
climb on top.

JOHN LATHAM

The Child's Tale

A Terrible Infant

I recollect a nurse called Ann,
    Who carried me about the grass,
And one fine day a fine young man
    Came up, and kissed the pretty lass.
She did not make the least objection!
    Thinks I, 'Aha!
    When I can talk I'll tell Mamma!'
– And that's my earliest recollection.

      FREDERICK LOCKER

Small Incident in Library

The little girl is lost among the books.
Two years old maybe, in bobble cap,
White lacy tights, red coat. She stands and looks.
'Can't see you, Mummy.' Mummy, next row up,
Intent on reading answers absently:
'I'm here, love.' Child calls out again: 'Can't see.'

A large man, his intentions of the best,
Stoops: 'Where's Mummy, then?' Child backs away.
Now the tall shelves threaten like a forest.
She toddles fast between them, starts to cry,
Takes the next aisle down and as her mother
Rounds one end disappears behind the other.

I catch the woman's tired-eyed prettiness.
We smile, shake heads. The child comes back in sight,
Hurtles to her laughing, hugs her knees:
'Found you!', in such ringing pure delight
It fills the room, there's no one left who's reading.
The mother looks down, blinking. 'Great soft thing.'

DAVID SUTTON

Letty's Globe

When Letty had scarce passed her third glad year,
And her young artless words began to flow,
One day we gave the child a coloured sphere
Of the wide earth, that she might mark and know,
By tint and outline, all its sea and land.
She patted all the world; old empires peeped
Between her baby fingers. Her soft hand
Was welcome at all frontiers. How she leaped,
And laughed, and prattled, in her world-wide bliss.
But when we turned her sweet unlearnèd eye
On our own isle, she raised a joyous cry,
'Oh! yes, I see it. Letty's home is there!'
And while she hid all England with a kiss,
Bright over Europe fell her golden hair.

CHARLES TENNYSON TURNER

Kindergarten

Sun is shining . . .

*Me dey ya in dis place wid dese strange faces. An' me
  alone.*

Sun is shining
me have tuppence in me pocket . . .

Me dey ya in dis place wid dese strange faces. An' me
alone.
An' me can't do wha me want. And me wan' go home.

Sun is shining
me have tuppence in me pocket
me have two banana . . .

Me dey ya in dis place wid dese strange faces. An' me
alone. An' me can't do wha' me want. An me wan' go
home.
Me muma leave me and gone far away. An' a wan' see her.
Me wan' go to market, me don't wan' be wid dese strange
people. Me wan' go home.

Sun is shining
me have tuppence in me pocket
me have two banana
me have ball . . .

But watchya now: we playing, we dancing, we singing. An'
de big people nice. Dem show me nice t'ings . . .

STANLEY MARTIN

Leaving School

I was eight when I set out into the world
wearing a grey flannel suit.
I had my own suitcase.
I thought it was going to be fun.

I wasn't listening
when everything was explained to us in the Library,
so the first night I didn't have any sheets.
The headmaster's wife told me
to think of the timetable as a game of 'Battleships'.
She found me walking around upstairs
wearing the wrong shoes.

I liked all the waiting we had to do at school,
but I didn't like the work.
I could only read certain things
which I'd read before, like the Billy Goat Gruff books,
but they didn't have them there.
They had the Beacon Series.
I said 'I don't know,'
then I started saying nothing.
Every day my name was read out
because I'd forgotten to hang something up.

I was so far away from home I used to forget things.
I forgot how to get undressed.
You're supposed to take off your shirt and vest
after you've put on your pyjama bottoms.
When the headmaster's wife came round for Inspection
I was fully dressed again, ready for bed.
She had my toothbrush in her hand
and she wanted to know why it was dry.
I was miles away, with my suitcase, leaving school.

                          HUGO WILLIAMS

The Game of Cricket

I wish you'd speak to Mary, Nurse,
She's really getting worse and worse.
Just now when Tommy gave her out
She cried and then began to pout
And then she tried to take the ball
Although she cannot bowl at all.
And now she's standing on the pitch,
The miserable little Bitch!

HILAIRE BELLOC

The Child's Tale

My Dad was just no good, so Mummy says
(and Mummy says she always tells the truth).
He upped and left us when I was a kid –
all right, a *smaller* kid – and Mummy says
he doesn't send her money (though he does,
because I've seen her cash the cheques). He sends
as much as he can manage, so *he* says –
but Mummy says he always tells us lies,
and Mummy always tells the truth, she says.
And we're both better off without him now,
so Mummy says. She says that he was cruel;
that he left *me*, not her. Can that be true?

She says he never helped her. But he did –
and I know that, but never dare to say.
And if he was the cruel one, then why
was he the one who seemed to be unhappy?
And why was she so pleased to see him cry?

(He did, sometimes; I saw him.) Anyway,
he only sees me when the lawyers let him.
(I've heard him call *them* Bastards – what are they?)
Mummy keeps telling me I must forget him –
but when he brings me home I know he's sad.
He says he loves me – but he tells me lies,
my Mummy says, and Mummy tells the truth.
He's selfish, unreliable and bad,
she says.
      I think I rather like my Dad.

ERIC MILLWARD

Good Boys Don't Cry

Turning from a window I would say
'Look Mummy . . .' and the place where
she had stood stared back
like air made solid with a presence.

Good boys don't cry. She will
remember she has left me here,
the air will thicken and return
her like a ghost to an old haunt.

I wait. Lap after lap is on a level
with my eyes, but if I bury
my head into a stranger
I will insult her and gain nothing.

Already I have learned not to want
the thing I want unless wanting
should place it out of reach, so now
I settle for something less than love:

wish only for the sight of her
still unaware that I have gone
so that I can follow quietly
keeping hidden until she turns

and, showing no surprise,
rejoin her quietly, taking
peace at her side as though
neither noticed the other gone.

But we are a long way from home
and perhaps even that want is bigger
than my share of the world. If I shout,
just raising my voice, will she mind?

'Mummy!' I try, but louder than
I intended and this sound frightens me;
it is out and I know Good Boys
Don't Cry but I cry

over and over until the tears make
the faces around me bright and broken.
In this rainbow questioning
my voice knows only one word

and I know I have lost her because
I tried too hard for her return . . .
until 'Booby!' and 'Watercart!' she yells
and both my ears begin to burn.

EDWIN BROCK

The Boot Man

'Thin as sliced bacon,' she would say, fingering
The soles. 'They're for the Boot Man.' And I'd go
Up Crab Lane, the slight wafer of words she doled
Me out with worrying my tongue. *Please, soled
And heeled by Saturday.*

                    She didn't know
That given speech, to me, refused to come.
I couldn't read aloud in class; sat dumb
In front of howling print; could never bring
On my bitched breath the words I should have said,
Though they were pummelling inside my head.

Somehow the Boot Man stanched my speeches more
Than all the rest. He'd watch me as I tried
To retch up words: his eyes a wash-tub blue,
Stork-head held sideways; braces threaded through
Loops in his long-johns. Once again my dead
Father stood there: army boots bright as glass,
Offering me a hand as colourless
As phosgene.

                And they told me time would cure
The irresolute tongue. But never said that I
Would meet again upon the faithless, sly
And every-morning page, the Boot Man's eye.

CHARLES CAUSLEY

Black Bottom

We're practising for the school show
I'm trying to do the Cha Cha and the Black Bottom
but I can't get the steps right
my right foot's left and my left foot's right
my teacher shouts from the bottom
of the class, come on show

us what you can do – I thought
you people had it in your blood.
My skin is hot as burning coal
like that time she said Darkies are like coal
in front of the whole class – my blood?
what does she mean? I thought

she'd stopped all that after the last time
my dad talked to her on parent's night
the other kids are allright till she starts
my feet step out of time, my heart starts
to miss beats like when I can't sleep at night
What Is In My Blood? The bell rings. It is time.

                                    JACKIE KAY

A Hereford Sampler

Sarah Bulmer, aged ten in 1835,
stitched the name Jesus before all others.
This was, I imagine, an idea of her mother's
or of *her* mother's who was doubtless alive

and very much so. If Sarah had friends
they were doing the same in similar homes –
Gratitude to Jesus was rife at that time
in embroidered script, each small hand

led by the guiding hand. Poor Sarah –
she paused sometimes, her tight lips
clenching the needle, thumbtip and fingertip
runnelled with labour. Oh Sarah,

what pride when you finished? What duty
done? Were you good then forever?
Stretched in its frame it doesn't look threadbare.
For what new task were you set free?

Whether for marriage or maidhood, I don't know.
These Hereford churchyards are weighty with stone.
Did you go far? I doubt it. If I left this room
and searched long enough I should probably find you.

JOHN MOLE

11 Plus

11 Plus

We spent all afternoon buying the uniform
Buying an entire list from blazer to vests
All crackle wrapped in paper and string
Under the whizzing of overhead tracks
And the chanting of my mother's Co-op number.

On our way home
She insisted that I learn to use a phone.
I still remember the weight of that door
As it sealed us in
The thin skitter of pages
The trick with coins and a dial
And my father's voice distant
Breathing a cheap perfume
All of us knowing but none of us saying
That the boy was going away.

MARTYN WILEY

Man Junior

I look over the bannisters and see, far down,
Miss Pyke taking Roll Call. I push my feet
into a pair of Cambridge house shoes
half my size and shuffle downstairs.
When I answer my name there is a long silence,
then Miss Pyke asks me where I've been.
I tell her I was reading a book
and didn't notice the time.

I see I have a smaller desk this term
as a punishment for being late.

I have to sit sideways, facing Armitage,
who eats little pieces of blotting paper
dipped in ink. When the bell goes
I barge off down Lower Corridor
with my head down and my elbows out,
knocking everyone flying.

Hurrah! There's a letter for me today.
I'd rather have a parcel, but I'm always happy
when I see the familiar blue envelope
propped on the mantelpiece
on the other side of School Hall.
I don't open it straight away, of course.
I shove it in my pocket
and read it later, like a man.

I'm standing outside the Headmaster's Study
waiting for the green light to come on.
Either I've failed Common Entrance
or my parents have died. When I go in
he's sitting at his desk, staring out the window.
For a long time we watch Sgt. Burrows
pushing his marker round Long Field,
Mr Harvey taking fielding practice.

The Headmaster pulls his writing case towards him
and opens it with his paper knife.
Inside is the worst news in the world,
my copy of Man Junior with a picture of a girl
in a bikini playing with a beach ball.
I must have left it under my mattress.
The Headmaster looks at me in disbelief
and asks, 'What is the meaning of this?'

HUGO WILLIAMS

Tich Miller

Tich Miller wore glasses
with elastoplast-pink frames
and had one foot three sizes larger than the other.

When they picked teams for outdoor games
she and I were always the last two
left standing by the wire-mesh fence.

We avoided one another's eyes,
stooping, perhaps, to re-tie a shoelace,
or affecting interest in the flight

of some fortunate bird, and pretended
not to hear the urgent conference:
'Have Tubby!' 'No, no, have Tich!'

Usually they chose me, the lesser dud,
and she lolloped, unselected,
to the back of the other team.

At eleven we went to different schools.
In time I learned to get my own back,
sneering at hockey-players who couldn't spell.

Tich died when she was twelve.

WENDY COPE

ortrait of Girl with Comic Book

Thirteen's no age at all. Thirteen is nothing.
It is not wit, or powder on the face,
Or Wednesday matinées, or misses' clothing,
Or intellect, or grace.
Twelve has its tribal customs. But thirteen
Is neither boys in battered cars nor dolls,
Not *Sara Crewe*, or movie magazines,
Or pennants on the walls.

Thirteen keeps diaries and tropical fish
(A month at most); scorns jump-ropes in the spring;
Could not, would fortune grant it, name its wish;
Wants nothing, everything;
Has secrets from itself, friends it despises;
Admits none to the terrors that it feels;
Owns half a hundred masks but no disguises;
And walks upon its heels.

Thirteen's anomalous — not that, not this:
Not folded bud, or wave that laps a shore,
Or moth proverbial from the chrysalis.
Is the one age defeats the metaphor.
Is not a town, like childhood, strongly walled
But easily surrounded; is no city.
Nor, quitted once, can it be quite recalled —
Not even with pity.

PHYLLIS MCGINLEY

The Conventionalist

Fourteen-year-old, why must you giggle and dote,
Fourteen-year-old, why are you such a goat?
I'm fourteen years old, that is the reason,
I giggle and dote in season.

STEVIE SMITH

Teenager

Her head is full of the idea
that the street is full
of her.

She is confidence, shyness
nun, coquette.

She cries silently
Look at me! Look at me! —
ready to fly at a glance.

She walks precisely,
as if the pavement
might peep up her skirt.

These are her mayfly days
when Alive is everything.
That they will pass
forever, and soon,
she does not know,
and this is happiness.

(This, too, she does not know.)

The field of her knowledge
is narrow
and covers everything.

She knows who rules the earth.

ERIC MILLWARD

Fifteen

South of the bridge on Seventeenth
I found back of the willows one summer
day a motorcycle with engine running
as it lay on its side, ticking over
slowly in the high grass. I was fifteen.

I admired all that pulsing gleam, the
shiny flanks, the demure headlights
fringed where it lay; I led it gently
to the road and stood with that
companion, ready and friendly. I was fifteen.

We could find the end of a road, meet
the sky on out Seventeenth. I thought about
hills, and patting the handle got back a
confident opinion. On the bridge we indulged
a forward feeling, a tremble. I was fifteen.

Thinking, back farther in the grass I found
the owner, just coming to, where he had flipped
over the rail. He had blood on his hand, was pale —

I helped him walk to his machine. He ran his hand
over it, called me good man, roared away.

I stood there, fifteen.

WILLIAM STAFFORD

Abigail

Abigail knew when she was born
Among the roses, she was a thorn.
Her quiet mother had lovely looks.
Her quiet father wrote quiet books.
Her quiet brothers, correct though pale,
Weren't really prepared for Abigail
Who entered the house with howls and tears
While both of her brothers blocked their ears
And both of her parents, talking low,
Said, 'Why is Abigail screaming so?'

Abigail kept on getting worse.
As soon as she teethed she bit her nurse,
At three, she acted distinctly cool
Toward people and things at nursery school.
'I'm sick of cutting out dolls,' she said,
And cut a hole in her dress, instead.
Her mother murmured, 'She's bold for three.'
Her father answered, 'I quite agree.'
Her brothers mumbled, 'We hate to fuss,
But *when* will Abigail be like us?'

Abigail, going through her teens,
Liked overalls and pets and machines.
In college, hating most of its features,

She told off all of her friends and teachers.
Her brothers, graduating from Yale,
Said: 'Really, you're hopeless, Abigail.'
And while her mother said, 'Fix your looks,'
Her father added, 'Or else write books.'
And Abigail asked, 'Is that a dare?'
And wrote a book that would curl your hair.

KAYE STARBIRD

The Rebel

When everybody has short hair,
The rebel lets his hair grow long.

When everybody has long hair,
The rebel cuts his hair short.

When everybody talks during the lesson,
The rebel doesn't say a word.

When nobody talks during the lesson,
The rebel creates a disturbance.

When everybody wears a uniform,
The rebel dresses in fantastic clothes.

When everybody wears fantastic clothes,
The rebel dresses soberly.

In the company of dog lovers,
The rebel expresses a preference for cats.

In the company of cat lovers,
The rebel puts in a good word for dogs.

When everybody is praising the sun,
The rebel remarks on the need for rain.

When everybody is greeting the rain,
The rebel regrets the absence of sun.

When everybody goes to the meeting,
The rebel stays at home and reads a book.

When everybody stays at home and reads a book,
The rebel goes to the meeting.

When everybody says, Yes please,
The rebel says, No thank you.

When everybody says, No thank you,
The rebel says, Yes please.

It is very good that we have rebels.
You may not find it very good to be one.

                              D. J. ENRIGHT

Little Johnny's Change of Personality

This afternoon
    while looking for hidden meanings in Superman
    And discussing tadpole collections
    I discovered I belonged to Generation X

And developed numerous complexes;
I turned on to Gothic fairytales and Alister Crowley,
Equated Batman with homosexuality, so

Please Mr Teacher, Sir,
Turn round from your blackboard,
The whole class has its hands up,
We're in rather a hurry.
The desks are returning to forests,
The inkwells overflowing,
The boys in the backrow have drowned.
Please Mr Teacher, Sir,
Turn round from your blackboard,
Your chalks are crumbling,
Your cane's decaying,
Turn round from your blackboard
We're thinking of leaving.

This afternoon
   a quiet criminal moves through the classroom
   Deciding on his future;
   Around him, things have fallen apart –
   Something's placed an inkstained finger
   On his heart.

                              BRIAN PATTEN

My First Cup of Coffee

I'm sophisticated in my Cuban heels,
my mother's blue felt hat
with the smart feather like a fishing fly

as I sit with her in the Kardomah; and
coffee please, I say, not orange squash,
crossing my legs, elegant as an advert.

Beyond the ridges of my mother's perm
the High Street is a silent film
bustling with extras: hands grasping purses,

steering prams, eyes fixed on lists,
bolster hips in safe-choice-coloured skirts
— and then, centre screen, Nicolette Hawkins

(best in the class at hockey, worst at French)
and a boy — kissing,
blouse straining, hands

where they shouldn't be:
the grown-up thing. My hat's hot, silly;
coffee tastes like rust.

My mother, following my gaze, frowns: common.
I'm thinking, if I could do all that
I could be bad at French.

CAROLE SATYAMURTI

Sonnet: In Time of Revolt

The Thing must End. I am no boy! I AM
    NO BOY!! being twenty-one. Uncle, you make
    A great mistake, a very great mistake,
In chiding me for letting slip a 'Damn!'
What's more, you called me 'Mother's one ewe lamb,'

Bade me 'refrain from swearing – for *her* sake –
  Till I'm grown up' . . . – By God! I think you take
Too much upon you, Uncle William!

You say I am your brother's only son.
I know it. And, 'What of it?' I reply.
My heart's resolvèd. *Something must be done.*
So shall I curb, so baffle, so suppress
This too avuncular officiousness,
Intolerable consanguinity.

                    RUPERT BROOKE

A Job of Some Sort

from A Serving-Maid

With merry lark this maiden rose,
And straight about the house she goes,
With swapping besom in her hand;
And at her girdle in a band
A jolly bunch of keys she wore;
Her petticoat fine laced before,
Her tail tucked up in trimmest guise,
A napkin hanging o'er her eyes,
To keep off dust and dross of walls,
That often from the windows falls . . .

She never sleepèd much by night,
But rose sometimes by candle-light
To card and spin, or sew her smock;
There could no sooner crow a cock,
But she was up, to sleek her clothes,
And would be sweet as any rose.
Full cleanly still the girl would go
And handsome in a house also,
As ever saw I country wench.
She sweeped under every bench,
And shaked the cushions in their kind;
When out of order she did find
A rush, a straw or little stick,
She could it mend, she was so quick
About her business every hour.

This maid was called her mistress' flower . . .
She was well made from top to tail;
Yea, all her limbs, withouten fail,
Were fine and feat. She had a hand,
There was no fairer in the land,

Save that with toil it changed hue.
Her fingers small, her veins full blue;
Her nails a little largely grown;
Her hair much like the sun it shone;
Her eyes as black as jet did seem;
She did herself full well esteem.
Her lips were red, but somewhat chapped.
Her tongue was still and seldom clapped.

THOMAS CHURCHYARD

from The Girl in the Baker's

We call her the girl in the baker's, though she's a girl no
    longer,
For she was a slip of a girl when we were boys.
We would stop
By her shop
And stare at her with the hunger
Of teenage hobbledehoys,
Amazed at the sight
Of a nymph or a sprite
Among cottage loaves, cheesecakes, and patties.
She didn't seem to belong
To the dull doughy world of those fatties
Her Pa and her Ma — when the girl in the baker's was
    young.

We call her the girl in the baker's; though she is nearer
Forty than thirty now, slab-faced and sour,
Satisfied rather than sorry when things get dearer;
Totting up bills, or writing an order for flour,
On purpose to keep you waiting. She does it to spite you
For having a husband or wife, or kids to delight you,

For being better off, better looking, for having more
Than Maisie – or merely for being happy though poor.

She cultivates little queues. Standing in one this morning,
Watching her taking her time over counting the change,
Adding a bill up three times, ostensibly yawning,
Then suddenly snapping at Mrs Green from The Grange
The single word 'Yes?' –
I was trying to guess
What had happened to change her,
To sour and estrange her,
What had gone wrong.
I tried to envisage her long, long, long
Ago:
The nymph among the dough,
The sprite that wantoned and winked at us teenage loons
With noses glued to her window, ogling
And oafishly goggling
At Maisie and macaroons.

It was rather like trying to remember
Cuckoo-call in December,
Flowers out of season.
Then suddenly, for some reason,
The shop fell still.
Maisie wrote slowly a bill.
Then looking as always vaguely, shortsightedly vexed,
She cried out: 'Next!'
The customer murmured something. Then Maisie's voice
    again
Came to me flat and dull and doughy and plain:
'The Fancies is all gone,' she said, oh pitifully bereft;
'The Fancies is all gone,' said Maisie. 'Only the Buns is
    left.'

JOHN MOORE

Trumpet Player

The Negro
With the trumpet at his lips
Has dark moons of weariness
Beneath his eyes
Where the smoldering memory
Of slave ships
Blazed to the crack of whips
About his thighs.

The Negro
With the trumpet at his lips
Has a head of vibrant hair
Tamed down,
Patent-leathered now
Until it gleams
Like jet —
Were jet a crown.

The music
From the trumpet at his lips
Is honey
Mixed with liquid fire.
The rhythm
From the trumpet at his lips
Is ecstasy
Distilled from old desire —

Desire
That is longing for the moon
Where the moonlight's but a spotlight
In his eyes,

Desire
That is longing for the sea
Where the sea's a bar-glass
Sucker size.

The Negro
With the trumpet at his lips
Whose jacket
Has a *fine* one-button roll,
Does not know
Upon what riff the music slips
Its hypodermic needle
To his soul —

But softly
As the tune comes from his throat
Trouble
Mellows to a golden note.

LANGSTON HUGHES

Knife-thrower's Girl

Then I was steel,
I was a dark glitter,
my indigo costume, the sequin one
was quiet, I was quiet,
felt that I was a long spring uncoiling
high up on one velvet and rhinestone heel.

Then flash, they flashed
left, right, down, left, right.
I smiled around, they buried themselves
too fast to be heard, there was I sweating
and breathing only to the front,

felt the mascara running on one eye,
and how I hankered for a wash.

Oh I could eat flowers,
my teeth are natural. Thud, thud.
Round my head. Candied roses.
The eight knives, my eight friends.
The boys are cheering. Walk about a bit.
The worst moment is the moving away.

PETER LEVI

The Lift Man

In uniform behold me stand,
The lovely lift at my command.
   I press the button: Pop,
And down I go below the town;
The walls rise up as I go down
   And in the basement stop.

For weeks I've worked a morning shift
On this old Waygood-Otis lift.
   And goodness, don't I love
To press the knob that shuts the gate
When customers are shouting 'Wait!'
   And soar to floors above.

I see them from my iron cage,
Their faces looking up in rage,
   And then I call 'First floor!'
'Perfume and ladies' underwear!'
'No sir, Up only. Use the stair.'
   And up again we soar.

The second floor for kiddie goods,
And kiddie-pantz and pixie-hoods,
     The third floor, restaurant:
And here the people always try
To find one going down, so I
     Am not the lift they want.

On the roof-garden floor alone
I wait for ages on my own
     High, high above the crowds.
O let them rage and let them ring,
For I am out of everything,
     Alone among the clouds.

JOHN BETJEMAN

Librarian

Girl in the library, with mousy hair
and dog-eared dress — whose life is filled with dates,
though never one to thrill you. — How long is it
since someone wanted to remove your jacket
and read the lettering along your spine?
Since last you stamped your foot instead of books?

By your books we would know you? I suspect
you could direct me to appropriate shelves,
to suitable works: those one-off books of verse
that daily share with you neglect and space,
collecting dust along their upper edges,
spending the unremitting days and nights
on the same shelf, being taken out once a year.

ERIC MILLWARD

Lady-Probationer

Some three, or five, or seven, and thirty years;
A Roman nose; a dimpling double-chin;
Dark eyes and shy that, ignorant of sin,
Are yet acquainted, it would seem, with tears;
A comely shape; a slim, high-coloured hand,
Graced, rather oddly, with a signet ring;
A bashful air, becoming everything;
A well-bred silence always at command.
Her plain print gown, prim cap, and bright steel chain
Look out of place on her, and I remain
Absorbed in her, as in a pleasant mystery.
Quick, skilful, quiet, soft in speech and touch . . .
'Do you like nursing?' 'Yes, Sir, very much.'
Somehow, I rather think she has a history.

W. E. HENLEY

The Lavatory Attendant

I counted two and seventy stenches
All well defined and several stinks!
              Coleridge

Slumped on a chair, his body is an S
That wants to be a minus sign.

His face is overripe Wensleydale
Going blue at the edges.

In overalls of sacerdotal white
He guards a row of fonts

With lids like eye-patches. Snapped shut
They are castanets. All day he hears

Short-lived Niagaras, the clank
And gurgle of canescent cisterns.

When evening comes he sluices a thin tide
Across sand-coloured lino,

Turns Medusa on her head
And wipes the floor with her.

WENDY COPE

The Betterwear Man

The Betterwear man
stands at the backdoor and knocks
but I will not let him in.
On the doorstep he opens his case, displays
brushes, stain-removers, pan-scrubs
to scour my soul – my soul *is* scoured
by that gentle voice:
'This cleans cleaner than clean, removes
stains from inside the cup.'

I never feel dingier
than when I say No
to the Betterwear Man –
his goods are so good,
better than best,
lasting longer than life.

He's no right to pester me
with persuasion, promises, free-gifts –
today a needle-threader
till I'm drawn through myself –
but most of all, pity
that plugs me with guilt.
He pleads as with a daughter,
and I shut the door in his face.

Now he's gone I'm all wrung out
like a dish-cloth of not-clean water.

PHOEBE HESKETH

The City

Business men with awkward hips
And dirty jokes upon their lips,
And large behinds and jingling chains,
And riddled teeth and riddling brains,
And plump white fingers made to curl
Round some anaemic city girl,
And so lend colour to the lives
And old suspicions of their wives.

Young men who wear on office stools
The ties of minor public schools,
Each learning how to be a sinner
And tell 'a good one' after dinner,
And so discover it is rather
Fun to go one more than father.
But father, son and clerk join up
To talk about the Football Cup.

JOHN BETJEMAN

Business Girls

From the geyser ventilators
Autumn winds are blowing down
On a thousand business women
Having baths in Camden Town.

Waste pipes chuckle into runnels,
Steam's escaping here and there,
Morning trains through Camden cutting
Shake the Crescent and the Square.

Early nip of changeful autumn,
Dahlias glimpsed through garden doors,
At the back precarious bathrooms
Jutting out from upper floors,

And behind their frail partitions
Business women lie and soak,
Seeing through the draughty skylight
Flying clouds and railway smoke.

Rest you there, poor unbelov'd ones,
Lap your loneliness in heat.
All too soon the tiny breakfast,
Trolley-bus and windy street!

JOHN BETJEMAN

Lord Finchley

Lord Finchley tried to mend the Electric Light
Himself.
        It struck him dead: And serve him right!
It is the business of the wealthy man
To give employment to the artisan.

HILAIRE BELLOC

The Gas Man Cometh

'Twas on a Monday morning
The gas man came to call.
The gas-tap wouldn't turn, I wasn't getting gas at all,
He tore out all the skirting-boards to try to find the main
And I had to call a carpenter to put them back again.

Oh, it all makes work for the working man to do.

'Twas on a Tuesday morning
The carpenter came round
He hammered and he chiselled and he said, 'Look what
   I've found!
Your joints are full of dry rot, but I'll put them all to
   rights.'
Then he nailed right through a cable and out went all the
   lights.

Oh, it all makes work for the working man to do.

'Twas on a Wednesday morning
The electrician came

He called me Mr Saunderson, which isn't quite my name,
He couldn't reach the fusebox without standing on the bin,
And his foot went through a window, so I called a glazier in.

Oh, it all makes work for the working man to do.

'Twas on a Thursday morning
The glazier came along,
With his blow-torch and his putty and his merry glazier
    song
And he put another pane in; it took no time at all
But I had to get a painter in to come and paint the wall.

Oh, it all makes work for the working man to do.

'Twas on a Friday morning
The painter made a start
With undercoats and overcoats, he painted every part
Every nook and every cranny, but I found when he had
    gone,
He'd painted over the gas tap and I couldn't turn it on!

On Saturday and Sunday they do no work at all
So 'twas on a Monday morning that the gas man came to
    call.

MICHAEL FLANDERS AND DONALD SWANN

Woman Work

I've got the children to tend
The clothes to mend
The floor to mop
The food to shop

Then the chicken to fry
The baby to dry
I got company to feed
The garden to weed
I've got the shirts to press
The tots to dress
The cane to be cut
I gotta clean up this hut
Then see about the sick
And the cotton to pick.

Shine on me, sunshine
Rain on me, rain
Fall softly, dewdrops
And cool my brow again.

Storm, blow me from here
With your fiercest wind
Let me float across the sky
'Til I can rest again.

Fall gently, snowflakes
Cover me with white
Cold icy kisses and
Let me rest tonight.

Sun, rain, curving sky
Mountain, oceans, leaf and stone
Star shine, moon glow
You're all that I can call my own.

MAYA ANGELOU

On a Tired Housewife

Here lies a poor woman who was always tired,
She lived in a house where help wasn't hired:
Her last words on earth were: 'Dear friends, I am going
To where there's no cooking, or washing, or sewing,
For everything there is exact to my wishes,
For where they don't eat there's no washing of dishes.
I'll be where loud anthems will always be ringing,
But having no voice I'll be quit of the singing.
Don't mourn for me now, don't mourn for me never,
I am going to do nothing for ever and ever.'

ANON.

What is He?

What is he?
— A man, of course.
Yes, but what does he do?
— He lives, and is a man.
Oh quite! but he must work. He must have a job of some
    sort.
— Why?
Because obviously he's not one of the leisured classes.
— I don't know. He has lots of leisure. And he makes quite
    beautiful chairs.
There you are then! He's a cabinet-maker.
— No, no!
Anyhow a carpenter and joiner.
— Not at all.
But you said so.
— What did I say?

That he made chairs, and was a joiner and carpenter.
— I said he made chairs, but I did not say he was a
  carpenter.
All right then, he's just an amateur.
— Perhaps! Would you say a thrush was a professional
  flautist, or just an amateur? —
I'd say it was just a bird.
— And I'd say he is just a man.
All right! You always did quibble.

D. H. LAWRENCE

Strangers on a Train

The Man in the Bowler Hat

I am the unnoticed, the unnoticeable man:
The man who sat on your right in the morning train:
The man you looked through like a windowpane:
The man who was the colour of the carriage, the colour of
    the mounting
Morning pipe smoke.

I am the man too busy with a living to live,
Too hurried and worried to see and smell and touch:
The man who is patient too long and obeys too much
And wishes too softly and seldom.

I am the man they call the nation's backbone,
Who am boneless – playable catgut, pliable clay:
The Man they label Little lest one day
I dare to grow.

I am the rails on which the moment passes,
The megaphone for many words and voices:
I am graph, diagram,
Composite face.

I am the led, the easily-fed,
The tool, the not-quite-fool,
The would-be-safe-and-sound,
The uncomplaining bound,
The dust fine-ground,
Stone-for-a-statue waveworn pebble-round.

A. S. J. TESSIMOND

Subway Station

This evening   Mr Howard T. Lewis,
of unknown address,   gloomy and tired,
wearing a grey overcoat and brown hat,
having decided to take   the BMT, Canarsie Line,
met   at the last station on 8th Ave.
a man   in a grey overcoat and brown hat
whose face,   gloomy and tired, was
the face of Mr   Howard T. Lewis,
while by the barrier   at the end of the empty platform
stood a man   in a grey overcoat, of gloomy appearance,
whose face   was also the face
of Howard T. Lewis   and   gazed dumbly
at the bottom of the dirty steps   down which came
a man in a brown hat,   gloomy and tired,
with a face that was the face of Howard T. Lewis.

And then   through the worn wooden spokes
of the turnstile   came a woman, tired and gloomy,
of unknown address   with a handbag and in a brown
hat   whose face was the face
of all men   and therefore also of Howard T. Lewis and
the steps in the distance   and the nervously muffled steps
near by, steps   of figures bowed by the murkiness
and pale from the light were the steps
of Howard T. Lewis, steps   from an unknown address
to   an unknown address,   now and then
the turnstile turned again   with a snap like a head
dropping in the basket,   or behind the barrier
could be seen   a figure without sex and of no
address,   but otherwise completely like
Howard T. Lewis,   steps   were heard,

heads, spokes, distances, lights and tunnels
sucked in the sign   8th Ave.   8th Ave.   8th Ave.
in droning crescendo.

When the train left   a stray wind
scattered the pages of a paper   in which there was a
   report on   the unknown
address,   fate   and identification
of a man   in a grey overcoat and brown hat,
gloomy and tired.

MIROSLAV HOLUB
(translated by Ian and Jarmila Milner)

Skanking Englishman Between Trains

Met him at Birmingham Station
small yellow hair Englishman
hi fi stereo swinging in one hand
walking in rhythm to reggae sound/Man

he was alive
he was full-o-jive
said he had a lovely
Jamaican wife

Said he couldn't remember
the taste of English food
I like mih drops
me johnny cakes
me peas and rice
me soup/Man

he was alive
he was full-o-jive
said he had a lovely
Jamaican wife

Said, showing me her photo
whenever we have a little quarrel
you know/to sweeten her up
I surprise her with a nice mango/Man

he was alive
he was full-o-jive
said he had a lovely Jamaican wife

GRACE NICHOLS

Canon Gloy

One morning, just as Canon Gloy
Was starting gaily for the station,
The Doctor said: 'Your eldest boy
Must have another operation!'
'What!' cried the Canon. 'Not again?
That's *twice* he's made me miss my train!'

HARRY GRAHAM

Inter-City
(for Anne Harvey)

Opposite me
a fat brown man
is crying
fat glass tears
on to his fair-isle pullover.

Needles of rain
mean-streak the landscape.
Bricks . . . allotments . . . bricks . . .
and the fat brown man
sits opposite me, crying.

Perhaps he thinks
no one will notice
if he keeps his eyes closed,
his face forced
into composure.

And everyone is
not noticing.
As for me,
I'm stringing the tears
into a narrative.

CAROLE SATYAMURTI

The Small Brown Nun

The small brown nun in the corner seat
Smiles out of her wimple and out of her window
Through thick round glasses and through the glass,
And her wimple is white and her habit neat
And whatever she thinks she does not show
As the train jerks on and the low fields pass.

The beer is warm and the train is late
And smoke floats out of the carriage window.
Crosswords are puzzled and papers read,
But the nun, as smooth as a just-washed plate,

Does nothing at all but smile as we go,
As if she listened to something said

Not here, or beyond, or out in the night,
A close old friend with a gentle joke
Telling her something through the window
Inside her head, all neat and right
And snug as the white bound round the yolk
Of a small brown egg in a nest in the snow.

ANTHONY THWAITE

Midnight on the Great Western

In the third-class seat sat the journeying boy,
    And the roof-lamp's oily flame
Played down on his listless form and face,
Bewrapt past knowing to what he was going,
    Or whence he came.

In the band of his hat the journeying boy
    Had a ticket stuck; and a string
Around his neck bore the key of his box,
That twinkled gleams of the lamp's sad beams
    Like a living thing.

What past can be yours, O journeying boy
    Towards a world unknown,
Who calmly, as if uncurious quite
On all at stake, can undertake
    This plunge alone?

Knows your soul a sphere, O journeying boy,
      Our rude realms far above,
Whence with spacious vision you mark and mete
This region of sin that you find you in,
            But are not of?

THOMAS HARDY

Conversation on a Train

I'm Shirley, she's Mary.
We're from Swansea
(if there was a horse there
it'd be a one-horse town
but there isn't even that).
We're going to Blackpool
Just the week. A bit late I know
But then there's the Illuminations
Isn't there? No, never been before.
Paris last year. Didn't like it.
Too expensive and nothing there really.

Dirty old train isn't it?
And not even a running buffet.
Packet of crisps would do
Change at Crewe
Probably have to wait hours
For the connection, and these cases
Are bloody heavy.
And those porters only want tipping.
Reminds you of Paris that does
Tip tip tip all the time.
Think you're made of money over there.

Toy factory, and Mary works in a shop.
Grocers. Oh it's not bad
Mind you the money's terrible.
Where are you from now?
Oh aye, diya know the Beatles then?
Liar!
And what do you do for a living?
You don't say.
Diya hear that Mary?
Well I hope you don't go home
And write a bloody poem about us.

ROGER MCGOUGH

The Negro Girl

Black delicate face
among a forest
of white pasty faces.

Her eyelids closed
for a moment only
as she stood by the door
of the subway car,

and in that instant
my lips had hurdled
the crowd and planted
the warmest of kisses
on those folded dark petals,

then vanished as quickly
before the quick eyes
could open to discover
her unknown impetuous
delirious lover.

RAYMOND SOUSTER

In a Station of the Metro

The apparition of these faces in the crowd;
Petals on a wet, black bough.

EZRA POUND

Faintheart in a Railway Train

At nine in the morning there passed a church,
At ten there passed me by the sea,
At twelve a town of smoke and smirch,
At two a forest of oak and birch,
      And then, on a platform, she:

A radiant stranger, who saw not me.
I said, 'Get out to her do I dare?'
But I kept my seat in my search for a plea,
And the wheels moved on. O could it but be
    That I had alighted there!

THOMAS HARDY

To a Fat Lady Seen from the Train

O why do you walk through the fields in gloves,
    Missing so much and so much?
O fat white woman whom nobody loves,
Why do you walk through the fields in gloves,
When the grass is soft as the breast of doves
    And shivering-sweet to the touch?
O why do you walk through the fields in gloves,
    Missing so much and so much?

FRANCES CORNFORD

The Fat White Woman
to Frances Cornford

Why do you rush through the fields in trains,
Guessing so much and so much;
Why do you flash through the flowery meads,
Fat-headed poet whom nobody reads;
And how do you know such a frightful lot
About people in gloves as such?

And how the devil can you be sure,
Guessing so much and so much,
How do you know but what someone who loves
Always to see me in nice white gloves
At the end of the field you are rushing by,
Is waiting for his Old Dutch?

G. K. CHESTERTON

Scene from a Slow Train

'Man in Armchair'
Glancing up from a tray
his face blue with news.

'Children on Bed'
A sparkling bounce
as heavy pillows swing.

'Woman with Plates'
Drawing from the froth
with pink gauntlets.

'About to Kiss'
She turns away
as he lowers his head.

Individually lit
Hanging
Against a black wall
As the rain falls.

MARTYN WILEY

Unforgettable – That Face

Hesitant

He sees beyond her face another face.
It is the one he wants.
He stares at it in amazement;
There is nothing anywhere quite like it.
There is nothing else that's wanted.

She sees beyond his face another face.
It stares at her in amazement.
She stares back, equally amazed.
Just why, she can't quite answer.
She simply wants it.

These faces have been waiting now
A long time to be introduced.
If only the faces in front
Would do something about it.

BRIAN PATTEN

Song

And would you see my mistress' face?
It is a flowery garden place
Where knots of beauties have such grace
That all is work and nowhere space.

It is a sweet delicious morn
Where day is breeding, never born.
It is a meadow yet unshorn
Which thousand flowers do adorn.

It is the heavens' bright reflex,
Weak eyes to dazzle and to vex;
It is the Idaea of her sex,
Envy of whom doth world perplex.

It is a face of death that smiles,
Pleasing though it kills the whiles,
Where death and love in pretty wiles
Each other mutually beguiles.

It is fair beauty's freshest youth,
It is the feigned Elysium's truth,
The Spring that wintered hearts reneweth;
And this is that my soul pursueth.

THOMAS CAMPION

Anne Boleyn
A Legend of the Tower of London

Her little feet in scarlet shoon
   They made a pleasant sound
Across the pavement where the moon
   Drew patterns on the ground.

Her clenchèd fists so small and white
   Went beating on the door,
The oaken door that to her sight
   Would open, never more.

She knelt upon the grey cold stone,
   And bowed her head in tears;
She wept, because her heart had grown
   Too wild to hide its fears.

'O Harry love, O dear my King
  I prithee let me in;
Thou couldst not do this cruel thing
  To merry Anne Boleyn.'

She fluttered like some wounded lark
  And ever called his name;
They chained her wrists and through the dark
  They led her to her shame.

So young was she to die alone,
  So fair, and full of tears,
So warm to rest beneath a stone
  Through countless weary years,

That sometimes now men hear her feet
  Across the tower floor,
Her voice beseech, her small hands beat
  Upon that silent door.

'O Harry love, O dear my King
  I prithee let me in;
Thou couldst not do this cruel thing
  To merry Anne Boleyn.'

BARBARA BINGLEY

The Dancer

'What was she like?' they asked, and then I knew
That I had never looked upon her face,
That I could tell them of her timeless grace,
Curve of the neck, light gesture of a hand;
The picture of a swallow's flight I drew,
And hoped, perhaps, that they might understand.

'What colour was her hair?' I do not know,
And yet I think it misted a white arm
And mingled with her dancing. There was charm
In every movement, and of all most sweet,
Most unforgotten wind-swept to and fro,
The leaf-blown motion of her elfin feet.

'Had her eyes beauty?' I cannot tell, alas!
I saw the magic in a changing dream . . .
A flash of silver on a wandering stream . . .
And I have kept for my remembering
How through the morning skies the wild swans pass,
And I recall the tremor of a wing.

CELIA RANDALL

Eighteenth Century Lady

*Her head was full of feathers, flowers, jewels and gewgaws
and as high as Lady Archer's; her dress was trimmed with
beads, silver, Persian sashes and all sort of fancies; her face
was thin and fiery, and her whole manner spoke a lady all
alive.*

FANNY BURNEY'S *Journal.*

Oh, she was a lady all alive!
She bedeviled the beaux
who would woo and wive;
she wore no sackcloth
and no ashes,
she wore beads
and Persian sashes.
She wore feathers
and fine fancies

going to routs
and plays and dances,
with gewgaws, whims
and silver dresses,
and pearls and curls
and twirls of tresses.
Her jewels shone
like midnight's marchers,
her hair built high
as Lady Archer's,
with brooches, wings
and wonders wiry.
Her witchy face
was fine and fiery.
Her hoop it nearly
spread an acre;
she was a credit
to her maker.
Her maker was pleased
he could contrive
such a lady,
a lady all alive.

ROSE O'NEILL

Sonnet: A Footballer

If I could paint you, friend, as you stand there,
Guard of the goal, defensive, open-eyed,
Watching the tortured bladder slide and glide
Under the twinkling feet; arms bare, head bare,
The breeze a-tremble through crow-tufts of hair;
Red-brown in face, and ruddier having spied
A wily foeman breaking from the side,

Aware of him, — of all else unaware:
If I could limn you, as you leap and fling
Your weight against his passage, like a wall;
Clutch him and collar him, and rudely cling
For one brief moment till he falls — you fall:
My sketch would have what Art can never give,
Sinew and breath and body; it would live.

EDWARD CRACROFT LEFROY

A Face

If one could have that little head of hers
    Painted upon a background of pale gold,
Such as the Tuscan's early art prefers!
    No shade encroaching on the matchless mould
Of those two lips, which should be opening soft
    In the pure profile; not as when she laughs,
For that spoils all: but rather as if aloft
    Yon hyacinth, she loves so, leaned its staff's
Burthen of honey-coloured buds to kiss
And capture 'twixt the lips apart for this.
Then her lithe neck, three fingers might surround,
How it should waver on the pale gold ground
Up to the fruit-shaped, perfect chin it lifts!
I know, Correggio loves to mass, in rifts
Of heaven, his angel faces, orb on orb
Breaking its outline, burning shades absorb:
But these are only massed there, I should think,
    Waiting to see some wonder momently
    Grow out, stand full, fade slow against the sky
    (That's the pale ground you'd see this sweet face by),
    All heaven, meanwhile, condensed into one eye
Which fears to lose the wonder, should it wink.

ROBERT BROWNING

In an Artist's Studio

One face looks out from all his canvases,
   One selfsame figure sits or walks or leans:
   We found her hidden just behind those screens,
That mirror gave back all her loveliness.
A queen in opal or in ruby dress,
   A nameless girl in freshest summer-greens,
   A saint, an angel – every canvas means
The same one meaning, neither more nor less.
He feeds upon her face by day and night,
   And she with true kind eyes looks back on him,
Fair as the moon and joyful as the light:
   Not wan with waiting, not with sorrow dim;
Not as she is, but was when hope shone bright;
   Not as she is, but as she fills his dream.

CHRISTINA ROSSETTI

Paint

A dumpy plain-faced child stands gazing there,
One hand laid lightly on a purple chair.
Her stuffed and stone-grey gown is laced with black;
A chain, with pendent star, hangs round her neck.
Red bows deck wrist and breast and flaxen hair;
Shoulder to waist's a band of lettered gold.
Round eyed, and cupid mouth – say, seven years old;
The ghost of her father in her placid stare.
Darkness beyond; bold lettering overhead:
LINFANTE. MARGUERITE, there I read;
And wondered – tongue-tied mite, and shy, no doubt –
What grave Velasquez talked to her about.

WALTER DE LA MARE

The Looking-Glass

Queen Bess was Harry's daughter!

The Queen was in her chamber, and she was middling old,
Her petticoat was satin and her stomacher was gold.
Backwards and forwards and sideways did she pass,
Making up her mind to face the cruel looking-glass.
    The cruel looking-glass that will never show a lass
    As comely or as kindly or as young as once she was!

The Queen was in her chamber, a-combing of her hair,
There came Queen Mary's spirit and it stood behind her
    chair,
Singing, 'Backwards and forwards and sideways may you
   pass,
But I will stand behind you till you face the looking-glass.
    The cruel looking-glass that will never show a lass
    As lovely or unlucky or as lonely as I was!'

The Queen was in her chamber, a-weeping very sore,
There came Lord Leicester's spirit and it scratched upon
    the door,
Singing, 'Backwards and forwards and sideways may you
    pass,
But I will walk beside you till you face the looking-glass.
    The cruel looking-glass that will never show a lass
    As hard and unforgiving or as wicked as you was!'

The Queen was in her chamber; her sins were on her head;
She looked the spirits up and down and statelily she said:
'Backwards and forwards and sideways though I've been,
Yet I am Harry's daughter and I am England's Queen!'

And she faced the looking-glass (and whatever else there
   was),
And she saw her day was over and she saw her beauty
   pass
In the cruel looking-glass that can always hurt a lass
More hard than any ghost there is or any man there was!

RUDYARD KIPLING

Lily Smalls
from *Under Milk Wood*

Oh there's a face!
Where you get that hair from?
Got it from an old tom cat.
Give it back then, love.
Oh there's a perm!

Where you get that nose from, Lily?
Got it from my father, silly.
You've got it on upside down!
Oh there's a conk!

Look at your complexion!
Oh no, *you* look.
Needs a bit of make-up.
Needs a veil.
Oh there's glamour!

Where you get that smile, Lil?
Never you mind, girl.
Nobody loves you.
That's what *you* think.

Who is it loves you?
Shan't tell.
Come on, Lily.
Cross your heart then?
Cross my heart.

DYLAN THOMAS

When You See Millions
of the Mouthless Dead

When you see millions of the mouthless dead
Across your dreams in pale battalions go,
Say not soft things as other men have said,
That you'll remember. For you need not so.
Give them not praise. For, deaf, how should they know
It is not curses heaped on each gashed head?
Nor tears. Their blind eyes see not your tears flow.
Nor honour. It is easy to be dead.
Say only this, 'They are dead.' Then add thereto,
'Yet many a better one has died before.'
Then, scanning all the o'ercrowded mass, should you
Perceive one face that you loved heretofore,
It is a spook. None wears the face you knew.
Great death has made all his for evermore.

CHARLES HAMILTON SORLEY

Strange Meeting

It seemed that out of battle I escaped
Down some profound dull tunnel, long since scooped
Through granites which titanic wars had groined.

Yet also there encumbered sleepers groaned,
Too fast in thought or death to be bestirred.
Then, as I probed them, one sprang up, and stared
With piteous recognition in fixed eyes,
Lifting distressful hands, as if to bless.
And by his smile, I knew that sullen hall, —
By his dead smile I knew we stood in Hell.
With a thousand pains that vision's face was grained;
Yet no blood reached there from the upper ground,
And no guns thumped, or down the flues made moan.
'Strange friend,' I said, 'here is no cause to mourn.'
'None,' said that other, 'save the undone years,
The hopelessness. Whatever hope is yours,
Was my life also; I went hunting wild
After the wildest beauty in the world,
Which lies not calm in eyes, or braided hair;
But mocks the steady running of the hour,
And if it grieves, grieves richlier than here.
For by my glee might many men have laughed,
And of my weeping something had been left,
Which must die now. I mean the truth untold,
The pity of war, the pity war distilled.
Now men will go content with what we spoiled,
Or, discontent, boil bloody, and be spilled.
They will be swift with swiftness of the tigress.
None will break ranks, though nations trek from progress.
Courage was mine, and I had mystery,
Wisdom was mine, and I had mastery:
To miss the march of this retreating world
Into vain citadels that are not walled.
Then, when much blood had clogged their chariot-wheels,
I would go up and wash them from sweet wells,
Even with truths that lie too deep for taint.
I would have poured my spirit without stint
But not through wounds; not on the cess of war.

Foreheads of men have bled where no wounds were.
I am the enemy you killed, my friend.
I knew you in this dark: for so you frowned
Yesterday through me as you jabbed and killed.
I parried; but my hands were loath and cold.
Let us sleep now . . .'

WILFRED OWEN

Framed in a First-Storey Winder . . .

Framed in a first-storey winder of a burnin' buildin'
Appeared: A Yuman Ead!
Jump into this net, wot we are 'oldin'
And yule be quite orl right!

But 'ee wouldn't jump . . .

And the flames grew Igher and Igher and Igher.
(Phew!)

Framed in a second-storey winder of a burnin' buildin'
Appeared: A Yuman Ead!
Jump into this net, wot we are 'oldin'
And yule be quite orl right!

But 'ee wouldn't jump . . .

And the flames grew Igher and Igher and Igher
(Strewth!)

Framed in a third-storey winder of a burnin' buildin'
Appeared: A Yuman Ead!

Jump into this net, wot we are 'oldin'
And yule be quite orl right!
Honest!

And 'ee jumped . . .

And 'ee broke 'is bloomin' neck!

ANON.

Unforgettable

Unforgettable
that face —
man in the street
laughing, police
dragging him off

ISHIKAWA TAKUBOBU
(translated by Carl Sesar)

Mrs Reece Laughs

Laughter, with us, is no great undertaking;
A sudden wave that breaks and dies in breaking.
Laughter, with Mrs Reece is much more simple:
It germinates, it spreads, dimple by dimple,
From small beginnings, things of easy girth,
To formidable redundancies of mirth.
Clusters of subterranean chuckles rise,
And presently the circles of her eyes
Close into slits, and all the woman heaves,
As a great elm with all its mounds of leaves

Wallows before the storm. From hidden sources
A mustering of blind volcanic forces
Takes her and shakes her till she sobs and gapes.
Then all that load of bottled mirth escapes
In one wild crow, a lifting of huge hands
And creaking stays, a visage that expands
In scarlet ridge and furrow. Thence collapse,
A hanging head, a feeble hand that flaps
An apron-end to stir an air and waft
A streaming face . . . And Mrs Reece has laughed.

MARTIN ARMSTRONG

Maude Ruggy

from *The Tunning of Elinor Rumming*

Maude Ruggy thither skipped:
She was ugly hipped,
And ugly thick lipped,
Like an onion sided,
Like tan leather hided:
She had her so guided
Between the cup and the wall
That she was there withall
Into a palsy fall:
With that her head shakèd,
And her handes quakèd,
One's head would have askèd
To see her naked.
She drank so of the dregs,
The dropsy was in her legs;
Her face glist'ring like glass,
All foggy fat she was:
She had also the gout
In all her joints about;

Her breath was sour and stale,
And smellèd all of ale:
Such a bedfellaw
Would make one cast his craw!

JOHN SKELTON

Peerless Jim Driscoll

I saw Jim Driscoll fight in nineteen ten.
That takes you back a bit. You don't see men
Like Driscoll any more. The breed's died out.
There's no one fit to lace his boots about.
All right son. Have your laugh. You know it all.
You think these mugs today that cuff and maul
Their way through ten or fifteen threes can fight:
They hardly know their left hand from their right.
But Jim, he knew; he never slapped or swung,
His left hand flickered like a cobra's tongue
And when he followed with the old one-two
Black lightning of those fists would dazzle you.
By Jesus he could hit. I've never seen
A sweeter puncher: every blow as clean
As silver. *Peerless Jim* the papers named him,
And yet he never swaggered, never bragged.
I saw him once when he got properly tagged –
A sucker punch from nowhere on the chin –
And he was hurt; but all he did was grin
And nod as if to say, 'I asked for that.'
No one was ever more worth looking at;
Up there beneath the ache of arc-lamps he
Was just like what we'd love our sons to be
Or like those gods you've heard about at school . . .
Well, yes, I'm old; and maybe I'm a fool.

I only saw him once outside the ring
And I admit I found it disappointing.
He looked just — I don't know — just ordinary,
And smaller, too, than what I thought he'd be:
An ordinary man in fact, like you or me.

VERNON SCANNELL

The Worst of All Loves

Where do they go, the faces, the people seen
In glances and longed for, who smile back
Wondering where the next kiss is coming from?

They are seen suddenly, from the top decks of buses,
On railway platforms at the tea machine,
When the sleep of travelling makes us look for them.

A whiff of perfume, an eye, a hat, a shoe,
Bring back vague memories of names,
Thingummy, that bloke, what's-her-name.

What great thing have I lost, that faces in a crowd
Should make me look at them for one I know,
What are faces that they must be looked for?

But there's one face, seen only once,
A fragment of a crowd. I know enough of her.
That face makes me dissatisfied with myself.

Those we secretly love, who never know of us,
What happens to them? Only this is known.
They will never meet us suddenly in pleasant rooms.

DOUGLAS DUNN

The Family Face

Heredity

I am the family face;
Flesh perishes, I live on,
Projecting trait and trace
Through time to times anon,
And leaping from place to place
Over oblivion.

The years-heired feature that can
In curve and voice and eye
Despise the human span
Of durance — that is I;
The eternal thing in man,
That heeds no call to die.

THOMAS HARDY

Aunt Sue's Stories

Aunt Sue has a head full of stories.
Aunt Sue has a whole heart full of stories.
Summer nights on the front porch
Aunt Sue cuddles a brown-faced child to her bosom
And tells him stories.

Black slaves
Working in the hot sun,
And black slaves
Walking in the dewy night,
And black slaves
Singing sorrow songs on the banks of a mighty river
Mingle themselves softly

In the flow of old Aunt Sue's voice,
Mingle themselves softly
In the dark shadows that cross and recross
Aunt Sue's stories.

And the dark-faced child, listening,
Knows that Aunt Sue's stories are real stories.
He knows that Aunt Sue never got her stories
Out of any book at all,
But that they came
Right out of her own life.

The dark-faced child is quiet
Of a summer night
Listening to Aunt Sue's stories.

LANGSTON HUGHES

Cousin Sidney

Dull as a bat, said my mother
of cousin Sidney in 1940 that time he tried
to break his garden swing, jumping on it,
size 12 shoes – at fifteen the tallest boy
in the class, taller than loping Dan Morgan
when Dan Morgan wore his father's top hat.

Duller than a bat, said my father
when hero Sidney lied about his age
to claim rough khaki, silly ass;
and soon, somewhere near Dunkirk,
some foreign corner was forever Sidney
though uncle would not believe it.

Missing not dead please God, please,
he said, and never bolted the front door,
never string taken from the letter box,
never the hall light off lest his one son
came home through a night of sleet
whistling, We'll meet again.

Aunt crying and raw in the onion air
of the garden (the unswinging empty swing)
her words on a stretched leash
while uncle shouted, Bloody Germans.
And on November 11th, two howls
of silence even after three decades

till last year, their last year,
when uncle and aunt also went missing,
missing alas, so that now strangers
have bolted their door and cut the string
and no one at all (the hall so dark)
waits up for Sidney, silly ass.

DANNIE ABSE

Family Feeling

My Uncle Alfred had the terrible temper.
Wrapped himself up in its invisible cloak.
When the mood was on his children crept from the
    kitchen.
It might have been mined. Not even the budgie spoke.

He was killed in the First World War in Mesopotamia.
His widow rejoiced, though she never wished him dead.
After three years a postcard arrived from Southampton.
'Coming home Tuesday. Alf,' was what it said.

His favourite flower he called the antimirrhinum.
Grew it instead of greens on the garden plot.
Didn't care much for children, though father of seven.
Owned in his lifetime nine dogs all called Spot.

At Carnival time he rode the milkman's pony.
Son of the Sheikh, a rifle across his knee.
Alf the joiner as Peary in cotton-wool snowstorms.
Secret in cocoa and feathers, an Indian Cree.

I recognized him once as the Shah of Persia.
My Auntie's front-room curtains gave him away.
'It's Uncle Alf!' I said, but his glance was granite.
'Mind your own business, nosey,' I heard him say.

I never knew just what it was that bugged him,
Or what kind of love a father's love could be.
One by one his children bailed out of the homestead.
'You were too young when yours died,' they explained to
    me.

Today, walking through St Cyprian's Church-yard
I saw where he lay in a box the dry colour of bone.
The grass was tamed and trimmed as if for a Sunday.
Seven antimirrhinums in a jar of stone.

                              CHARLES CAUSLEY

The Spitfire on the Northern Line

Harry was an uncle. I saw him twice.
Both times he was a sailor home from war.
First, he arrived one morning, thumped the door,
Annoying old Ma Brown on the second floor,
And brought me two string-bags click-full of marbles.
In the grey light of that wartime dawn we lay
On the cold lino, rumbling zig-zag balls
Of colour to all corners of the room,
Until Ma Brown banged up at us with her broom.
I felt like a god in heaven, playing with thunder.
The second time, we went by Underground
To see his mother, my grandma. In all
That packed and rocking tube-train, down we sat
Together on the dirty wooden slats
Between the feet of passengers, and began
To build a Spitfire. He would send me off
Toddling with tininess against the sway
Of the train to fetch a propeller, then the wheels,
While like a Buddha crosslegged, all in blue,
He sat and bashed a nail or sank a screw.
And before the eyes of all, a Spitfire grew
And finally (a stop before the Angel)
He cried 'It's finished!' and the whole coachful
Shouted 'Hooray!'
                              Never, never again
Did I see Harry. Somewhere he was killed
And they slipped his body softly to the sea.
Thousands died that war. Most, like Harry,
Not distinguished by the enemies gunned down,
But remembered by some child.
                              I see it still,
That Spitfire on the Northern Line, nose-up,

Blotched with its camouflage, and gleaming bright,
And all those faces laughing with delight.

Uncle Roderick

His drifter swung in the night
from a mile of nets
between the Shiants and Harris.

My boy's eyes watched
the lights of the fishing fleet – fireflies
on the green field of the sea.

In the foc's'le he gave me a bowl
of tea, black, strong and bitter,
and a biscuit you hammered
in bits like a plate.

The fiery curtain came up
from the blackness, comma'd with corpses.

Round Rhu nan Cuideagan
he steered for home, a boy's god
in seaboots. He found his anchorage
as a bird its nest.

In the kitchen he dropped
his oilskins where he stood.

He was strong as the red bull.
He moved like a dancer.
He was a cran of songs.

NORMAN MACCAIG

For My Sister

'I'm too old to play with you any more' –
The words mean laughter now. But did I care?
Your dozen years to my ten did no more
Than make me stubborn in my games. You were

A figure dwindling, lost among real babies,
Pushing prams, a little mother then
And I, when ill, would find you back again
Wheeling me round. Yes, you were everybody's

Nurse when they were broken, worn, afraid
But I was King of cross-roads, theatres, farms,
Vigilant, a lord of what I'd made,
Sometimes the rigid soldier bearing arms,
Sometimes a look-out on all thorough-fares.

'I'm too old . . .' You do not seem so now,
Seem yourself made perfect, and indeed
Matriarch, grandmother, careful wife,
Queen over sickness, and you come and go
Busy with all that makes a newborn life,
Fast and thorough. I'm the child still slow.

ELIZABETH JENNINGS

Three Brothers

I had Three Brothers,
Harold and Robert and James,
All of them tall and handsome,

All of them good at games.
And I was allowed to field for them,
To bowl to them, to score:
I was allowed to slave for them
For ever and evermore.
Oh, I was allowed to fetch and carry for my Three
    Brothers,
Jim and Bob and Harry.

All of my brothers,
Harry and Jim and Bob,
Grew to be good and clever,
Each of them at his job.
And I was allowed to wait on them,
To be their slave complete,
I was allowed to work for them
And life for me was sweet,
For I was allowed to fetch and carry for my Three
    Brothers,
Jim and Bob and Harry.

Jim went out to South Africa,
Bob went out to Ceylon,
Harry went out to New Zealand
And settled in Wellington.
And the grass grew high on the cricket-pitch,
And the tennis-court went to hay,
And the place was too big and too silent
After they went away.

So I turned it into a Guest House,
After our parents died,
And I wrote to the boys every Sunday,
And once a year they replied.
All of them married eventually,

I wrote to their wives, of course,
And their wives wrote back on postcards –
Well . . . it might have been very much worse.

And now I have nine nieces,
Most of them home at school.
I have them all to stay here
For the holidays, as a rule.
And I am allowed to slave for them,
To do odd jobs galore,
I am allowed to work for them
And life is sweet once more,
For I am allowed to fetch and carry for the children of
Jim and Bob and Harry.

                    JOYCE GRENFELL

Have You Been to London?

'Have you been to London?'
My grandmother asked me.
                              'No.' –
China dogs on the mantelshelf,
Paper blinds at the window,
Three generations simmering on the bright black lead,
And a kettle filled to the neb,
Spilled over long ago.

I blew into the room, threw
My scholarship cap on the rack;
Wafted visitors up the flue
With the draught of my coming in –
Ready for Saturday's mint imperials,
Ready to read

The serial in *Titbits*, the evangelical
Tale in the parish magazine,
Under the green
Glare of the gas,
Under the stare of my grandmother's Queen.

My grandmother burnished her sleek steel hair —
Not a tooth in her jaw
Nor alphabet in her head,
Her spectacles lost before I was born,
Her lame leg stiff in the sofa corner,
Her wooden crutch at the steady:
'They shut doors after them
In London,' she said.

I crossed the hearth and thumped the door *to*;
Then turned to Saturday's stint,
My virtuosity of print
And grandmother's wonder:
Reading of throttler and curate,

Blood, hallelujahs and thunder.
While the generations boiled down to one
And the kettle burned dry
In a soon grandmotherless room;

Reading for forty years,
Till the print swirled out like a down-catch of soot
And the wind howled round
A world left cold and draughty,
Un-latched, un-done,
By all the little literate boys
Who hadn't been to London.

NORMAN NICHOLSON

Grammer's Shoes

I do seem to zee Grammer as she did use
Vor to show us, at Chris'mas, her weddèn shoes,
An' her flat spreadèn bonnet so big an' roun'
As a girt pewter dish a-turn'd upside down;
    When we all did draw near
    In a cluster to hear
O' the merry wold soul how she did use
To walk an' to dance wi' her high-heel shoes.

She'd a gown wi' girt flowers lik' hollyhocks,
An' zome stockèns o' gramfer's a-knit wi' clocks,
An' a token she kept under lock an' key, —
A small lock ov his heäir off avor 't wer grey.
    An' her eyes wer red,
    An' she shook her head,
When we'd all a-look'd at it, an' she did use
To lock it away wi' her weddèn shoes.

She could tell us such teäles about heavy snows,
An' o' raïns an' o' floods when the waters rose
All up into the housen, an' carr'd awoy
All the bridge wi' a man an' his little bwoy;
    An' o' vog an' vrost,
    An' o' vo'k a-lost,
An' o' peärties at Chris'mas, when she did use
Vor to walk hwome wi' gramfer in high-heel shoes.

Ev'ry Chris'mas she lik'd vor the bells to ring,
An' to have in the zingers to heär em zing
The wold carols she heärd many years a-gone,
While she warm'd em zome cider avore the bron';

An' she'd look an' smile
        At our dancèn, while
She did tell how her friends now a-gone did use
To reely wi' her in their high-heel shoes.

Ah! an' how she did like vor to deck wi' red
Holly-berries the window an' wold clock's head,
An' the clavy wi' boughs o' some bright green leaves,
An to meäke twoast an' eäle upon Chris'mas eves;
        But she's now, drough greäce,
        In a better pleäce.
Though we'll never vorget her, poor soul, nor lose
Gramfer's token ov heäir, nor her weddèn shoes.

                        WILLIAM BARNES

Hot Summer Sunday

Especially on hot summer Sundays
my Grandpa liked to rest
supine in the narrow bathtub
soaking in curved cool water
sometimes flipping his toes
or, quite child-like,
toying with a pale green soapcake,
but mostly
staying motionless, eyes closed,
lips half-smiling,
limbs outstretched.

That hot summer Sunday
when I looked at him
straightly lying, lips parted,
silent in the shallow trough,

a foam of white, frothed and lacy,
set as new suds
about his shaven jawbones,
it seemed he might stir,
whistle a relaxed sigh,
unclose those eyelids,
ask me to scrub his back.

                    A. L. HENDRIKS

My Mother's Father

The sepia playbill,
faded, slightly torn,
proclaims you
VOCAL COMEDIAN,
the photo signed
'Sincerely yours,
Joe Humphreys.'

'Have starred' it says,
'In all principal towns.'
SPLENDID ENUNCIATION
and GOOD VOICE.
It doesn't name
the songs you used to sing.

At Tottenham Music Hall
twice-nightly,
not on Sundays,
your act would be
slick, dapper, jaunty,
hiding a darker side.

And Sundays, after lunch,
table pushed back,
we'd all join in:
'WHERE did you get that hat?
Where DID you get that hat?'
I turn back to your photo

Where masks of comedy and tragedy
recall your shifting moods.
Those I've inherited.
But could I claim the motto
on your playbill:

ALWAYS A SUCCESS
WITHOUT VULGARITY...?

ANNE HARVEY

It's Mother, You See

It's mother, you see.

I cannot fold her up like a pram or a bicycle.
It's every day crawling around the agencies.
I cannot leave her alone in a furnished room.
She has to come with me, arm in arm, umbrella'd,
Or trailing a little.

She is thin in wind and limb,
She is not quite white in the head,
Now and then she stops – suddenly and completely
Like a mutinous dog on a lead.

(And once, long ago, in reverse,
I trailed after *her* skirts in the throng streets,
Her basket of goodies
Bobbing just out of my reach)

She's no need to stare at the shops.
We have plenty more clothes, if we bothered to open the
    cases,
And hundreds of photographs of the way things were.
Sometimes we take out a bit of the better china
And wash it and put it away again.

It is every day to the agents,
Then on to the library, checking the papers for ads.
Or walking the streets, looking for signs that might say
Where to apply for a key.

It is hard on the legs, it is hard on the wits and the heart,
But I cannot leave her alone in a furnished room.
O come *on*, Mum. One day we'll find us a home
Somewhere this side of the sky.

                              ELMA MITCHELL

Gardening Gloves

Mild, knob-jointed, old,
They lie on the garage floor.
Scarred by the turn of a spade
In hard, agricultural wear
And soiled by seasonal mould
They *look* like animal skins –
Or imagine a gargoyle's hands.

But not my hands I'd swear,
Being large, rough and uncouth;
Yet the moment I pick them up
They assume an absurd truth,
They assert I have given them shape,
Making my hands the mirror
For their comfortable horror.

And I know if I put them on
I gain a deliberate skill,
An old, slow satisfaction
That is not mine at all
But sent down from other men.
Yes, dead men live again
In my reluctant skin.

I remember my father's hands,
How they moved as mine do now
While he took his jokes from the air
Like precise, comical birds.
These gloves are my proper wear.
We all preserve such lives.
I'm not sorry to have these gloves.

LESLIE NORRIS

Well Caught

These days I'm in love with my face.
It has grown round and genial as I've become older.
In it I see my grandfather's face and that
Of my mother. Yes — like a ball it has been thrown
From one generation to the next.

GERDA MAYER

The Lives of Other People

The Hunched

They will not leave me, the lives of other people,
I wear them near my eyes like spectacles.
The sullen magnates, hunched into chins and overcoats
In the back seats of their large cars;
The scholars, so conscientious, as if to escape
The things too real, the names too easily read,
Preferring language stuffed with difficulties;
And the children, furtive with their own parts;
The lonely glutton in the sunlit corner
Of an empty Chinese restaurant;
The coughing woman, leaning on a wall,
Her wedding ring finger in her son's cold hand,
In her back the invisible arch of death.
What makes them laugh, who lives with them?

I stooped to lace a shoe, and they all came back,
Dull, mysterious people without names or faces,
Whose lives I guess about, whose dangers tease,
And not one of them has anything at all to do with me.

DOUGLAS DUNN

Peasant Woman: Rhodes

These are my scarves and veils and boots of sweat.
My hands are horny with the donkey's straps.
I have not borne a living baby yet:
The one inside me may be strong perhaps.
In all this heat I wear thick wool. Beneath,
At least one slip I do not often change.

And if I smile I show my metal teeth,
But I must smile because you are so strange!
You smile back too. You came to have a look
And show your photos when you end your trip.
You seem to live by writing in a book.
We live off what we get from this dry land.
You understand, and leave a decent tip
But here, you see, we do not understand.

JOHN FULLER

The Road to Kerity

Do you remember the two old people we passed on the
    road to Kerity,
Resting their sack on the stones, by the drenched wayside,
Looking at us with their lightless eyes through the driving
    rain, and then out again
To the rocks, and the long white line of the tide:
Frozen ghosts that were children once, husband and wife,
    father and mother,
Looking at us with those frozen eyes; have you ever seen
    anything quite so chilled or so old?
        But we – with our arms about each other,
            We did not feel the cold!

CHARLOTTE MEW

from A Winchester Mosaic

A smell of cut grass and growing nettles.
Ducklings, hatched a week ago
that boldly range the bourne.

Among lime trees, the pale yellow
of a solitary street lamp left on,
dying in the light of leaves.

An old lady dressed in brown
who showers bread to a circle
of ducks pressed against her feet

and draws me in with her
'Aren't they nice?' as she turns
a delighted, open face.

JEREMY HOOKER

Old Man Travelling

The little hedgerow birds,
That peck along the road, regard him not.
He travels on, and in his face, his step,
His gait, is one expression: every limb,
His look and bending figure, all bespeak
A man who does not move with pain, but moves
With thought – He is insensibly subdued
To settled quiet: he is one by whom
All effort seems forgotten; one to whom
Long patience hath such mild composure given
That patience now doth seem a thing of which
He hath no need. He is by nature led
To peace so perfect that the young behold
With envy what the Old Man hardly feels.

WILLIAM WORDSWORTH

Another Small Incident

November evening, rain outside and dark
Beyond the building's honeycomb of warmth.
The old man stands there, waiting to be noticed.
He wears propitiation like a coat.
The girl looks up at him. 'Yes? Can I help you?'
'This card you sent like, that's the problem, see.
It says I've got your book, but that's not right.
I mean, I had it but I brought it back.
That's what I do, I read one, bring it back.
I never keep them, see.'
                              He stands, condemned
Yet quivering for justice. 'All right, sir.'
She smiles at him. 'We get mistakes like that.
Just leave the card with me.' He stares at her,
Seventy, with spotted hands, afraid,
And someone smiles at him and calls him sir.
Lighting at the contact, like a bulb,
He warms to her. 'That's what I do, you see.
I take the one, I read it, bring it back.
I thought, you know, it might be on the shelves.
I mean, if no one's had it since like, see.'
Another girl comes by. 'We're closing, Sue.
You coming?' Sue looks up and rolls her eyes.
The old man catches it. He understands.
He turns and shuffles out into the night.

DAVID SUTTON

To the Lady Behind Me

Dear Madam, you have seen this play;
I never saw it till today.
You know the details of the plot,
But, let me tell you, I do not.
The author seeks to keep from me
The murderer's identity,
And you are not a friend of his
If you keep shouting who it is.
The actors in their funny way
Have several funny things to say,
But they do not amuse me more
If you have said them just before;
The merit of the drama lies,
I understand, in some surprise,
But the surprise must now be small
Since you have just foretold it all.
The lady you have brought with you
Is, I infer, a half-wit too,
But I can understand the piece
Without assistance from your niece.
In short, foul woman, it would suit
Me just as well if you were mute;
In fact, to make my meaning plain,
I trust you will not speak again.
And – may I add one human touch? –
Don't breathe upon my neck so much.

A. P. HERBERT

To the Gentleman in Row E

Dear Sir, we in Row E are well aware
Your soul is steeped in music to the core.
You love, we notice, each succeeding air
More deeply than the one which came before.

You lead the orchestra in perfect time,
With ever-nodding head you set the pace,
We in Row E consider it a crime
You are not in Sir Thomas Beecham's place.

Your lily hands most delicately haver,
Each phrase is ended with a graceful twist,
You know, it seems, each breve and semi-quaver,
And play them gently on your other wrist.

Sometimes you hum the least familiar portions,
And beat upon the floor a faint tattoo,
Though we can stand a lot of your contortions,
We shouldn't tap too much if we were you!

Dear Sir, we need no musical instructor,
We also sang in oratorio,
And if you were a really good conductor,
Our lightning would have struck you hours ago!

VIRGINIA GRAHAM

Missing

Lonely in London is an endless story,
Tired in the sun on the District Line,
With Baron's Court baked beans opened in Ealing,
Tossing in bed and staring at the ceiling,
And: 'Yes, Mr Holdsworth, I'll put you through.'
A lot of work and not much glory
And a letter to Mum that says you're fine.

You played me songs on your piana.
Its E was missing like a tooth.

It always rained when I came to see you,
Rained like the mint, the window creaked with rain.
You sat in the window and I told you the truth.

Lonely in London is an endless story.
Where did you go to? Who do you see?
I played at being with you, yes I'm sorry.
Now in this dog's soup I'm less than me,
Miss you, your piana, your piana and your cardigan,
Miss you on Friday, miss you on Monday,
Your cardigan, your tears and the baked-bean smells.
You're like a secret that nobody tells,
Lonely in London, somewhere, now.

JOHN FULLER

At a Country Fair

At a bygone Western country fair
I saw a giant led by a dwarf
With a red string like a long thin scarf;
How much he was the stronger there
    The giant seemed unaware.

And then I saw that the giant was blind,
And the dwarf a shrewd-eyed little thing;
The giant, mild, timid, obeyed the string
As if he had no independent mind,
    Or will of any kind.

Wherever the dwarf decided to go
At his heels the other trotted meekly,
(Perhaps – I know not – reproaching weakly)
Like one Fate bade that it must be so,
    Whether he wished or no.

Various sights in various climes
I have seen, and more I may see yet,
But that sight never shall I forget,
And have thought it the sorriest of pantomimes,
    If once, a hundred times!

THOMAS HARDY

from The Prelude

How oft, among those overflowing streets
Have I gone forward with the crowd, and said
Unto myself, 'The face of every one
That passes by me is a mystery.'

WILLIAM WORDSWORTH

Summer Sales

LESS LUST
LESS PASSION
FOR THE HEALTHIER LIFE
EAT NUTS

A scarecrow of a man proclaimed
in sunny, lunchtime Oxford Street,
balancing the poster-pole
on words half-murmured to himself.

Fixed in expansive summer, women
lusting after any bargains
focussed their astonishment,
ranging the stare that fixed his face.
Lovers, propping passion on
each other's arms, smiled disbelief.
Blimey! He thinks we're monkeys! Laughter.

An unimpassioned constable,
his lust contained in uniform
of measured tread, came pacing in.

Move on, he said; *you can't stop here* . . .
(as if the man were anywhere)
Get moving. Come now. On your way.

The man moved on. But, as he passed,
I heard his toneless whispering.
John Smith, John Smith, John Smith, John Smith;
a lost voice crying its own name.

MAURICE LINDSAY

Counting the Mad

This one was put in a jacket,
This one was sent home,
This one was given bread and meat
But would eat none,
And this one cried No No No No
All day long.

This one looked at the window
As though it were a wall,
This one saw things that were not there,
This one things that were,
And this one cried No No No No
All day long.

This one thought himself a bird,
This one a dog,
And this one thought himself a man,
An ordinary man,
And cried and cried No No No No
All day long.

DONALD JUSTICE

Q

I join the queue
We move up nicely.

I ask the lady in front
What are we queuing for.
'To join another queue,'
She explains.

'How pointless,' I say,
'I'm leaving.' She points
To another long queue
'Then you must get in line.'

I join the queue.
We move up nicely.

ROGER MCGOUGH

People

I like people quite well
at a little distance.
I like to see them passing and passing
and going their own way,
especially if I see their aloneness alive in them.
Yet I don't want them to come near.
If they will only leave me alone
I can still have the illusion that there is room enough in the
    world.

D. H. LAWRENCE

Only One of Me

Every Day in Every Way

(Dr Coue: Every day in every way
I grow better and better)

When I got up this morning
I thought the whole thing through:
Thought, Who's the hero, the man of the day?
Christopher, it's you.

With my left arm I raised my right arm
High above my head:
Said, Christopher, you're the greatest.
Then I went back to bed.

I wrapped my arms around me,
No use counting sheep.
I counted legions of myself
Walking on the deep.

The sun blazed on the miracle,
The blue ocean smiled:
We like the way you operate,
Frankly, we like your style.

Dreamed I was in a meadow,
Angels singing hymns,
Fighting the nymphs and shepherds
Off my holy limbs.

A girl leaned out with an apple,
Said, You can taste for free.
I never touch the stuff, dear,
I'm keeping myself for me.

Dreamed I was in heaven,
God said, Over to you,
Christopher, you're the greatest!
And Oh, it's true, it's true!

I like my face in the mirror,
I like my voice when I sing.
My girl says it's just infatuation –
I know it's the real thing.

KIT WRIGHT

Telephone Conversation

The price seemed reasonable, location
Indifferent. The landlady swore she lived
Off premises. Nothing remained
But self-confession. 'Madam,' I warned,
'I hate a wasted journey – I am African.'
Silence. Silenced transmission of
Pressurized good-breeding. Voice, when it came,
Lipstick coated, long gold-rolled
Cigarette-holder pipped. Caught I was, foully.
'HOW DARK?' . . . I had not misheard . . . 'ARE YOU
   LIGHT
OR VERY DARK?' Button B. Button A. Stench
Of rancid breath of public hide-and-speak.
Red booth. Red pillar-box. Red double-tiered
Omnibus squelching tar. It *was* real! Shamed
By ill-mannered silence, surrender
Pushed dumbfoundment to beg simplification.
Considerate she was, varying the emphasis –
'ARE YOU DARK? OR VERY LIGHT?' Revelation came.
'You mean – like plain or milk chocolate?'

Her assent was clinical, crushing in its light
Impersonality. Rapidly, wave-length adjusted,
I chose. 'West African sepia' – and as afterthought,
'Down in my passport.' Silence for spectroscopic
Flight of fancy, till truthfulness clanged her accent
Hard on the mouthpiece. 'WHAT'S THAT?' conceding
'DON'T KNOW WHAT THAT IS.' 'Like brunette.'
'THAT'S DARK, ISN'T IT?' 'Not altogether.
Facially, I am brunette, but, madam, you should see
The rest of me. Palm of my hand, soles of my feet
Are a peroxide blond. Friction, caused –
Foolishly, madam – by sitting down, has turned
My bottom raven black – One moment, madam!' –
   sensing
Her receiver rearing on the thunderclap
About my ears – 'Madam,' I pleaded, 'wouldn't you rather
See for yourself?'

WOLE SOYINKA

Smart-boy

I am the Lad: the wide-awake, the smart-boy,
The one who knows the ropes and where he's going,
The easy smiler with the easy money.

I was the kid who got no praise or prizes
Who's now the man to get the peachbloom lovelies:
Black Market Boy with my good mixer manner.

I'm your tall talker in the fug of bar-rooms,
Quick at a deal, an old hand on the dog tracks,
Knowing in clubs, stander at Soho corners.

Go-between guy, I'm wiser than to work for
What the world hands me on a shiny salver,
Me the can't-catch-me-dozing razor-sharp-boy

Ready to set my toe to Order's backside:
Big-shot-to-be, big-city up-and-comer:
Quickstepper, racer, ace among you sleepers.

                    A. S. J. TESSIMOND

Stealing

The most unusual thing I ever stole? A snowman.
Midnight. He looked magnificent; a tall, white mute
beneath the winter moon. I wanted him, a mate
with a mind as cold as the slice of ice
within my own brain. I started with the head.

Better off dead than giving in, not taking
what you want. He weighed a ton; his torso,
frozen stiff, hugged to my chest, a fierce chill
piercing my gut. Part of the thrill was knowing
that children would cry in the morning. Life's tough.

Sometimes I steal things I don't need. I joy-ride cars
to nowhere, break into houses just to have a look.
I'm a mucky ghost, leave a mess, maybe pinch a camera.
I watch my gloved hand twisting the doorknob.
A stranger's bedroom. Mirrors. I sigh like this – *Aah*.

It took some time. Reassembled in the yard,
he didn't look the same. I took a run
and booted him. Again. Again. My breath ripped out
in rags. It seems daft now. Then I was standing
alone amongst lumps of snow, sick of the world.

Boredom. Mostly I'm so bored I could eat myself.
One time, I stole a guitar and thought I might
learn to play. I nicked a bust of Shakespeare once,
flogged it, but the snowman was strangest.
You don't understand a word I'm saying, do you?

CAROL ANN DUFFY

The Fiddler of Dooney

When I play on my fiddle in Dooney,
Folk dance like a wave of the sea;
My cousin is priest in Kilvarnet,
My brother in Mocharabuiee.

I passed my brother and cousin:
They read in their books of prayer;
I read in my book of songs
I bought at the Sligo fair.

When we come at the end of time
To Peter sitting in state,
He will smile on the three old spirits,
But call me first through the gate;

For the good are always the merry,
Save by an evil chance,
And the merry love the fiddle,
And the merry love to dance:

And when the folk there spy me,
They will all come up to me,
With 'Here is the fiddler of Dooney!'
And dance like a wave of the sea.

W. B. YEATS

Warning

When I am an old woman I shall wear purple
With a red hat which doesn't go, and doesn't suit me,
And I shall spend my pension on brandy and summer
  gloves
And satin sandals, and say we've no money for butter.
I shall sit down on the pavement when I'm tired
And gobble up samples in shops and press alarm bells
And run my stick along the public railings
And make up for the sobriety of my youth.
I shall go out in my slippers in the rain
And pick the flowers in other people's gardens
And learn to spit.

You can wear terrible shirts and grow more fat
And eat three pounds of sausages at a go
Or only bread and pickle for a week
And hoard pens and pencils and beermats and things in
  boxes.

But now we must have clothes that keep us dry
And pay the rent and not swear in the street
And set a good example for the children.
We must have friends to dinner and read the papers.

But maybe I ought to practise a little now?
So people who know me are not too shocked and surprised
When suddenly I am old and start to wear purple.

JENNY JOSEPH

The Fifth Sense

A 65-year-old Cypriot Greek shepherd, Nicolis Loizou, was wounded by security forces early today. He was challenged twice; when he failed to answer, troops opened fire. A subsequent hospital examination showed that the man was deaf. News Item, December 30th, 1957.

Lamps burn all the night
Here, where people must be watched and seen,
And I, a shepherd, Nicolis Loizou,
Wish for the dark, for I have been
Sure-footed in the dark, but now my sight
Stumbles among these beds, scattered white boulders,
As I lean towards my far slumbering house
With the night lying upon my shoulders.

My sight was always good,
Better than others. I could taste wine and bread
And name the field they spattered when the harvest
Broke. I could coil in the red
Scent of the fox out of a maze of wood
And grass. I could touch mist, I could touch breath.
But of my sharp senses I had only four.
The fifth one pinned me to my death.

The soldiers must have called
The word they needed: Halt. Not hearing it,
I was their failure, relaxed against the winter
Sky, the flag of their defeat.
With their five senses they could not have told
That I lacked one, and so they had to shoot.
They would fire at a rainbow if it had
A colour less than they were taught.

Christ said that when one sheep
Was lost, the rest meant nothing any more.
Here in this hospital, where others' breathing
Swings like a lantern in the polished floor
And squeezes those who cannot sleep,
I see how precious each thing is, how dear,
For I may never touch, smell, taste or see
Again, because I could not hear.

PATRICIA BEER

Sonnet

Thus am I mine own prison. Everything
Around me free and sunny and at ease:
Or if the shadow, in a shade of trees
Which the sun kisses, where the gay birds sing
And where all winds make various murmuring;
Where bees are found, with honey for the bees;
Where sounds are music, and where silences
Are music of an unlike fashioning.
Then gaze I at the merrymaking crew,
And smile a moment and a moment sigh,
Thinking, Why can I not rejoice with you?
But soon I put the foolish fancy by:
I am not what I have nor what I do;
But what I was I am, I am even I.

CHRISTINA ROSSETTI

I Am

I am – yet what I am, none cares or knows;
    My friends forsake me like a memory lost:
I am the self-consumer of my woes –
    They rise and vanish in oblivions host,
Like shadows in love frenzied stifled throes
    And yet I am, and live – like vapours tost

Into the nothingness of scorn and noise,
    Into the living sea of waking dreams,
Where there is neither sense of life nor joys,
    But the vast shipwreck of my life's esteems;
Even the dearest that I love the best
    Are strange – nay, rather, stranger than the rest.

I long for scenes where man hath never trod,
    A place where woman never smiled or wept,
There to abide with my Creator God,
    And sleep as I in childhood sweetly slept,
Untroubling and untroubled where I lie,
    The grass below, above, the vaulted sky.

JOHN CLARE

Sonnet 29

When in disgrace with Fortune and men's eyes,
I all alone beweep my outcast state,
And trouble deaf heaven with my bootless cries,
And look upon myself and curse my fate,
Wishing me like to one more rich in hope,
Featur'd like him, like him with friends possess'd,

Desiring this man's art, and that man's scope,
With what I most enjoy contented least;
Yet in these thoughts myself almost despising,
Haply I think on thee, and then my state,
Like to the lark at break of day arising
From sullen earth, sings hymns at heaven's gate;
For thy sweet love remembered such wealth
  brings
That then I scorn to change my state with kings.

WILLIAM SHAKESPEARE

One

Only one of me
and nobody can get a second one
from a photocopy machine.

Nobody has the fingerprints I have.
Nobody can cry my tears, or laugh my laugh
or have my expectancy when I wait.

But anybody can mimic my dance with my dog.
Anybody can howl how I sing out of tune.
And mirrors can show me multiplied
many times, say, dressed up in red
or dressed up in grey.

Nobody can get into my clothes for me
or feel my fall for me, or do my running.
Nobody hears my music for me, either.

I am just this one.
Nobody else makes the words
I shape with sound, when I talk.

But anybody can act how I stutter in a rage.
Anybody can copy echoes I make.
And mirrors can show me multiplied
many times, say, dressed up in green
or dressed up in blue.

JAMES BERRY

The Old Familiar Faces

Archie and Tina

Archie and Tina
Where are you now,
Playmates of my childhood,
Brother and sister?

When we stayed in the same place
With Archie and Tina
At the seaside,
We used

To paddle the samphire beds, fish
Crabs from the sea-pool, poke
The anemones, run,
Trailing the ribbon seaweed across the sand to the sea's
    edge
To throw it in as far as we could. We dug
White bones of dead animals from the sandhills, found
The jaw-bone of a fox with some teeth in it, a stoat's skull,
The hind leg of a hare.

Oh, if only; oh if only!

Archie and Tina
Had a dog called Bam. The silver-sand
Got in his long hair. He had
To be taken home.

Oh, if only . . . !

One day when the wind blew strong
Our dog, Boy, got earache. He had
To be taken home in a jersey.

Oh what pleasure, what pleasure!

There never were so many poppies as there were then,
So much yellow corn, so many fine days,
Such sharp bright air, such seas.

Was it necessary that
Archie and Tina, Bam and Boy,
Should have been there too?
Yes, then it was. But to say now:

Where are you today
Archie and Tina,
Playmates of my childhood,
Brother and sister? Is no more than to say:

I remember
Such pleasure, so much pleasure.

STEVIE SMITH

About Friends

The good thing about friends
is not having to finish sentences.

I sat a whole summer afternoon with my friend once
on a river bank, bashing heels on the baked mud
and watching the small chunks slide into the water
and listening to them – plop plop plop.
He said 'I like the twigs when they . . . you
    know . . .
like that.' I said 'There's that branch . . .'

We both said 'Mmmm.' The river flowed and
    flowed
and there were lots of butterflies, that afternoon.

I first thought there was a sad thing about friends
when we met twenty years later.
We both talked hundreds of sentences,
taking care to finish all we said,
and explain it all very carefully,
as if we'd been discovered in places
we should not be, and were somehow ashamed.

I understood then what the river meant by flowing.

BRIAN JONES

The Mad Maid's Song

Good morrow to the day so fair;
    Good morning, sir, to you:
Good morrow to mine own torn hair
    Bedabbled with the dew.

Good morning to this primrose, too;
    Good morrow to each maid
That will with flowers the tomb bestrew,
    Wherein my love is laid.

Ah! woe is me; woe, woe is me!
    Alack and welladay!
For pity, sir, find out that bee,
    Which bore my love away.

I'll seek him in your bonnet brave;
    I'll seek him in your eyes;
Nay, now I think they've made his grave
    I' the bed of strawberries.

I'll seek him there; I know, ere this,
The cold, cold earth doth shake him;
But I will go, or send a kiss
    By you, sir, to awake him.

Pray hurt him not; though he be dead,
    He knows well who do love him,
And who with green-turfs rear his head,
    And who do rudely move him.

He's soft and tender (pray take heed),
    With bands of cowslips bind him;
And bring him home. But 'tis decreed,
    That I shall never find him.

ROBERT HERRICK

Epitaph on Salathiel Pavy
A Child of Queen Elizabeth's Chapel

Weep with me, all you that read
    This little story;
And know, for whom a tear you shed,
    Death's self is sorry.
'Twas a child, that so did thrive
    In grace, and feature,
As *Heaven* and *Nature* seem'd to strive
    Which own'd the creature.

Years he numbered scarce thirteen
    When *Fates* turn'd cruel,
Yet three fill'd *Zodiacks* had he been
    The stage's jewel;
And did act (what now we moan)
    Old men so duly,
As, sooth, the *Parcae* thought him one,
    He play'd so truly.
So, by error, to his fate
    They all consented;
But viewing him since (alas, too late)
    They have repented.
And have sought (to give new birth)
    In baths to steep him;
But, being so much too good for earth,
    Heaven vows to keep him.

BEN JONSON

A Recollection

My father's friend came once to tea.
He laughed and talked. He spoke to me.
But in another week they said
That friendly pink-faced man was dead.

'How sad . . .' they said, 'the best of men . . .'
So I said too, 'How sad'; but then
Deep in my heart I thought, with pride,
'I know a person who has died.'

FRANCES CORNFORD

Epitaph

Here lies my wife,
   In earthy mould,
Who, when she lived,
   Did naught but scold.
Good friends go softly
   In your walking
Lest she should wake
   And rise up talking.

Ponteland,
Northumberland.

ANON.

Notting Hill Polka

We've – had –
A Body in the house
   Since Father passed away:
He took bad on
Saturday night an' he
   Went the followin' day:

Mum's – pulled –
The blinds all down
   An' bought some Sherry Wine,
An' we've put the tin
What the Arsenic's in
   At the bottom of the Ser-pen-tine!

W. BRIDGES-ADAMS

Epitaph on Charles II

Here lies a Great and Mighty King,
    Whose Promise none rely'd on,
He never said a Foolish thing
    Nor ever did a Wise one.

JOHN WILMOT,
EARL OF ROCHESTER

Richard Cory

Whenever Richard Cory went down town,
    We people on the pavement looked at him:
He was a gentleman from sole to crown,
    Clean favored, and imperially slim.

And he was always quietly arrayed,
    And he was always human when he talked;
But still he fluttered pulses when he said,
    'Good morning,' and he glittered when he walked.

And he was rich – yes, richer than a king –
    And admirably schooled in every grace:
In fine, we thought that he was everything
    To make us wish that we were in his place.

So on we worked, and waited for the light,
    And went without the meat, and cursed the bread;
And Richard Cory, one calm summer night,
    Went home and put a bullet through his head.

EDWARD ARLINGTON ROBINSON

Twins

Who finally never spoke in their place
On the side of the hill
— Small gestures did, nothing was left to say —
Old Howie and Merran his twin,
Questing about the hill all day like bees,
And he would go to the crags
Each morning, over the very face
For a clutch of eggs
(He liked a gull's egg fried among his bread)
And she to the burn with her pail
And maybe, on Mondays, rinse a tub of clothes;
First home would take the froth from the new ale,
Or turn in the press a wet white cheese,
But never a word said
— On such a tranquil wheel their time was spun —
Died on the same day.
They brought to the honeycomb bright brimming mouths.

GEORGE MACKAY BROWN

Women He Liked

Women he liked, did shovel-bearded Bob,
Old Farmer Hayward of the Heath, but he
Loved horses. He himself was like a cob,
And leather-coloured. Also he loved a tree.

For the life in them he loved most living things,
But a tree chiefly. All along the lane
He planted elms where now the stormcock sings
That travellers hear from the slow-climbing train.

Till then the track had never had a name
For all its thicket and the nightingales
That should have earned it. No one was to blame.
To name a thing beloved man sometimes fails.

Many years since, Bob Hayward died, and now
None passes there because the mist and the rain
Out of the elms have turned the lane to slough
And gloom, the name alone survives, Bob's Lane.

EDWARD THOMAS

Arracombe Wood

Some said, because he wud'n spaik
Any words to women but Yes and No,
Nor put out his hand for Parson to shake
He mun be bird-witted. But I do go
By the lie of the barley that he did sow,
And I wish no better thing than to hold a rake
Like Dave, in his time, or to see him mow.

Put up in churchyard a month ago,
'A bitter old soul,' they said, but it wadn't so.
His heart were in Arracombe Wood where he'd used to go
To sit and talk wi' his shadder till sun went low,
Though what it was all about us'll never know.
And there baint no mem'ry in the place
Of th' old man's footmark, nor his face;
Arracombe Wood do think more of a crow –
'Will be violets there in the Spring: in Summer time the
spider's lace;

And come the Fall, the whizzle and race
Of the dry, dead leaves when the wind gies chase;
And on the Eve of Christmas, fallin' snow.

CHARLOTTE MEW

Timer

Gold survives the fire that's hot enough
to make you ashes in a standard urn.
An envelope of coarse official buff
contains your wedding ring which wouldn't burn.

Dad told me I'd to tell them at St James's
that the ring should go in the incinerator.
That 'eternity' inscribed with both their names is
his surety that they'd be together, 'later'.

I signed for the parcelled clothing as the son,
the cardy, apron, pants, bra, dress –

the clerk phoned down: *6-8-8-3-1*?
Has she still her ring on? (Slight pause) *Yes!*

It's on my warm palm now, your burnished ring!

I feel your ashes, head, arms, breasts, womb, legs,
sift through its circle slowly, like that thing
you used to let me watch to time the eggs.

TONY HARRISON

The Old Familiar Faces

I have had playmates, I have had companions,
In my days of childhood, in my joyful school-days,
All, all are gone, the old familiar faces.

I have been laughing, I have been carousing,
Drinking late, sitting late, with my bosom cronies,
All, all are gone, the old familiar faces.

I loved a love once, fairest among women:
Closed are her doors on me, I must not see her –
All, all are gone, the old familiar faces.

I have a friend, a kinder friend has no man;
Like an ingrate, I left my friend abruptly;
Left him, to muse on the old familiar faces.

Ghost-like I paced round the haunts of my childhood,
Earth seemed a desert I was bound to traverse,
Seeking to find the old familiar faces.

Friend of my bosom, thou more than a brother,
Why wert not thou born in my father's dwelling?
So might we talk of the old familiar faces –

How some they have died, and some they have left me,
And some are taken from me; all are departed;
All, all are gone, the old familiar faces.

CHARLES LAMB

Index of First Lines

Acknowledgements

The editor and publishers gratefully acknowledge the following, for permission to reproduce copyright poems in this book:

'Cousin Sidney' by Dannie Abse, reprinted from *Collected Poems 1948 – 1976* (Century Hutchinson Ltd) by permission of Anthony Sheil Associates Ltd; 'Woman Work' by Maya Angelou reprinted from *And Still I Rise* by permission of Virago Press; 'Mrs Reece Laughs' by Martin Armstrong reprinted from the *Collected Poems* (Martin, Secker & Warburg Ltd) by permission of The Peters, Fraser & Dunlop Group Ltd; 'The Fifth Sense' by Patricia Beer reprinted from the *Collected Poems* by permission of Carcanet Press; 'The Game of Cricket' and 'Lord Finchley' by Hilaire Belloc reprinted from *Complete Belloc* by permission of Gerald Duckworth & Co Ltd; 'One' copyright © James Berry, 1988 from *When I Dance* (Hamish Hamilton Children's Books, 1988); 'The Lift Man' by John Betjeman from the *Uncollected Poems*, and 'The City' and 'Business Girls' by John Betjeman from the *Collected Poems*, reprinted by permission of John Murray (Publishers) Ltd; 'Good Boys Don't Cry' by Edwin Brock reprinted from *Here Now Always* (Martin, Secker & Warburg Ltd) by permission of David Higham Associates Ltd; 'The Bootman' by Charles Causley reprinted from *Secret Destination* (Macmillan) and 'Family Feeling' by Charles Causley, reprinted from *A Field of Vision* (Macmillan) by permission of David Higham Associates Ltd; 'Tich Miller' and 'The Lavatory Attendant' by Wendy Cope, reprinted from *Making Cocoa for Kingsley Amis* by permission of Faber and Faber Ltd; 'To A Fat Lady Seen from the Train' and 'A Recollection' by Frances Cornford from the *Collected Poems* by permission of Century Hutchinson Ltd; 'The Worst of All Loves' by Douglas Dunn from *Terry Street* and 'The Hunched' by Douglas Dunn from *The Happier Life*, reprinted by permission of Faber & Faber Ltd; 'Stealing' by Carol Ann Duffy, copyright © Carol Ann Duffy, 1987, reprinted from *Selling Manhattan* by permission of Anvil Press Poetry; 'The Rebel' by D. J. Enright, copyright © D. J. Enright, 1974, from *Rhyme Times Rhyme* (Chatto & Windus Ltd) reprinted by permission of Watson, Little Ltd; 'The Gas Man Cometh' by Michael Flanders and Donald Swann from *At the Drop of Another Hat* by Flanders & Swann, reproduced by permission of Claudia Flanders; 'Missing' by John Fuller reprinted from

Martin, 1985, from *Where I Am Coming From* (Akira Press); 'The Child's Tale', 'Teenager' and 'Librarian' by Eric Millward, reprinted from *Appropriate Noises* by permission of Peterloo Poets; 'Subway Station' by Miroslav Holub reprinted by permission of Bloodaxe Books Ltd from *The Fly* by Miroslav Holub, translated by Ian and Jarmila Milner (Bloodaxe Books, 1987); 'It's Mother, You See' by Elma Mitchell reprinted from *Furnished Rooms* by permission of Peterloo Poets; 'A Hereford Sampler' by John Mole, reprinted from *A Partial Light* (J. M. Dent & Sons Ltd); by permission of the author; extract from 'After the Christening' by Ogden Nash reprinted by permission of Curtis Brown Ltd; 'Skanking Englishman Between Trains' by Grace Nichols, reprinted from *The Fat Black Woman's Poems* by permission of Virago Press; 'Have You Been to London?' by Norman Nicholson reprinted from the *Collected Poems* (Faber & Faber Ltd), by permission of David Higham Associates Ltd; 'Gardening Gloves' by Leslie Norris reprinted from the *Selected Poems* by permission of Seren Books; 'Eighteenth Century Lady' by Rose O'Neill, copyright © 1970 by The New York Times Company, reprinted by permission; 'Little Johnny's Change of Personality' by Brian Patten from *Little Johnny's Confession* and 'Hesitant' by Brian Patten from *Storm Damage* reprinted by permission of Unwin Hyman Ltd; 'In a Station of the Metro' by Ezra Pound, reprinted from the *Collected Shorter Poems* by permission of Faber & Faber Ltd; 'Sister' and 'My First Cup of Coffee' by Carole Satyamurti, copyright © Carole Satyamurti, 1987, reprinted from *Broken Moon* by Carole Satyamurti (1987) by permission of Oxford University Press; 'Inter-City' by Carole Satyamurti, copyright © Carole Satyamurti, 1989, reprinted by permission of the author; 'Peerless Jim Driscoll' by Vernon Scannell reprinted by permission of the author; 'Unforgettable' by Ishikawa Takubobu, translation by Carl Sesar reprinted from *Poems to Eat* by permission of Kodansha International Ltd; 'The Conventionalist' from 'Two in One', and 'Archie and Tina' by Stevie Smith reprinted from *The Collected Poems of Stevie Smith* (Penguin Modern Classics) by permission of James MacGibbon; 'The Negro Girl' by Raymond Souster reprinted from *Collected Poems of Raymond Souster* by permission of Oberon Press; 'Fifteen' by William Stafford, copyright © William Stafford, 1964, reprinted from *Stories That Could Be True* by permission of Harper & Row, Publishers, Inc.; 'Abigail' by Kaye Starbird, copyright © Kaye Starbird, 1968, from *The Pheasant on Route Seven* (J. B. Lippincott Co.); 'Small Incident in the Library' and 'Another Small Incident' by David Sutton, reprinted from *Flints* by permission of Peterloo Poets; 'The Man in the Bowler Hat' and 'Smart

Boy' by A. S. J. Tessimond reprinted from *Collected Poems* (White-knights Press), by permission of Hubert Nicholson; 'Lily Smalls' by Dylan Thomas reprinted from *Under Milk Wood* (J. M. Dent & Sons Ltd) by permission of David Higham Associates Ltd; 'The Small Brown Nun' by Anthony Thwaite, reprinted from the *Collected Poems* (Martin, Secker & Warburg Ltd) by permission of Curtis Brown Ltd; 'On the Birth of His Son' by Su Tung-p'o, translation by Arthur Waley, reprinted by permission of Alison Waley; '11 Plus' and 'Scene from a Slow Train' by Martyn Wiley, reprinted by permission of the author; 'Leaving School' and 'Man Junior' by Hugo Williams, copyright © Hugo Williams, 1989, reprinted from Hugo Williams' *Selected Poems* (1989) by permission of Oxford University Press; 'My Baby Has No Name Yet' by Kin-Nam-Jo, translation copyright © Ko Won, 1970 from *Contemporary Korean Poetry* (University of Iowa Press); 'Every Day in Every Way' by Kit Wright from *Looked Over the Mountain* (Salamander Press), reprinted by permission of the author.

Every effort has been made to trace copyright holders, but in a few cases this has proved impossible. The editor and publishers apologize for these cases of unwilling copyright transgression and would like to hear from any copyright holders not acknowledged.

Also in Puffin

SHADOW DANCE
ed. Adrian Rumble

In the twilight world of this collection, Adrian Rumble has brought together a wonderful variety of poems – some written especially for this anthology – for children of all ages. Creatures of the night and of the imagination lurk within its pages, while other poets evoke the particular atmospheres of snowy, rainy or windy nights. Contributors include such traditional favourites as R. L. Stevenson and Walter de la Mare and modern poets such as Charles Causley, Mike Harding, Ted Hughes and Jack Prelutsky.

BEFORE YOU GO TO BED
Akister Finola

Pets and other animals feature strongly in this collection of poems, as do familiar childhood subjects as teddy bears, playing in the bath, and the horrors of being made to eat up your greens. Witty nonsense poems and comic narratives complete what is bound to become a favourite book with the younger age groups.

ALL TOGETHER NOW!
Tony Bradman

There are lots of lively, funny poems here about friends, television, food, birthdays, families, cats, school – amidst them wanders Grim Griselda the Grumpy Dragon, and George who pops his head round the page and interrupts other poems. An original and lively book which makes poetry great fun to read.

MR BIDERY'S SPIDERY GARDEN
David McCord

There are lots of interesting creatures hiding in this delightful collection of verse for younger children. Everything from snails and grasshoppers to waltzing mice and coolibahs are just waiting to be discovered amongst the grass and leaves of Mr Bidery's spidery garden. With plenty of fun, rhythm and rhyme, this is a book no one will be able to resist.

NAILING THE SHADOW
Roger McGough

Here is a book for everyone who loves to play with words and ideas. Stylish and entertaining, it is an unbeatable book by one of our top poets.

WHISPERS FROM A WARDROBE
Richard Edwards

Wonderful and exciting things happen in Richard Edwards' book of poems for younger readers. Cushions and coat hangers talk, and Nittles and Bubberlinks make friends. And did you know that there are people who breathe through one ear and people with back to front knees? Enter a world where nothing is impossible and the incredible is always true.